DAYS
AGLOW

DAYS AGLOW

Carla Holtermann

Fleming H. Revell Company
Old Tappan, New Jersey

Contents

Preface

Recently, the title of a Bible study course, "Life at Its Best," set a chain of thoughts in motion in my mind. I began to ask myself, "When is life really at its best? When is it aglow?"

The answer took shape slowly but definitely: life is at its best when every facet of life, every moment of life, every relationship of life, every undertaking of life—yes, even the consummation of life—is kindled with light and love from above.

The result of my search is this book. It is, however, only a beginning to my quest, for there is no final chapter in the study of life.

CARLA HOLTERMANN

I
Every Facet of Life

1
YEARNING FOR GOD

Our human lives are meant to be radiant, like diamonds whose lights glitter from every tiny facet. God wants to invade us and give us a glow. Created by a Master Builder, redeemed by a loving Saviour, indwelt by the empowering Spirit, we should show a sparkle from at least one facet every day—some gladness in Christ!

Think of the manifold facets of your life; your outer life and your inner life; your seeing, hearing, touching; your thinking, feeling, desiring; your creating, working, worshiping, playing; your helping, serving, suffering; your self-expression and response. With all this potential, are you living to your fullest? Are there deep unsatisfied longings in your heart? Retreat groups use these two questions to prepare participants for an honest and deepening experience. Never yet has any one, in any of my groups, admitted that he lives life to its fullest. All have expressed an honest yearning to increase their capacities to live—to have their lives count for more.

Asked if they could put these longings into words, the overall desire has been for "a deeper fellowship with Christ, deeper devotion to Him, more awareness of His Presence, more power to live effective Christian lives."

We begin this book with the premise that life at its best—

life aglow—begins in the Presence of Christ. Alone, we fumble and fail; with Him, we advance. He is the Light. If, daily, we are near Him, as within the arc of a candle's light, we see things in a clear perspective. When we are beyond that arc we are in semidarkness, or total darkness, depending upon how far we have wandered away from Him.

The invitation to come to Him is ever new; He will give meaning to life. The writer to the Hebrews urges us, "Let us go right in, to God Himself, with true hearts fully trusting Him to receive us . . ." (Hebrews 10:22, LIVING LETTERS). If you yearn for life at its best, begin now—come into the presence of your Saviour.

Some readers may ask, "What do you mean by that? How do I do this? Where do I begin?" A good place to begin is to get away from the pressures of your duties for a while, to be alone and still. Come apart into a place of hallowed stillness, some spot where you can enjoy the consciousness that you are alone—the privacy of your room, a quiet lake side, a garden bench, a country road, a church bench when no one else is there, or the altar—anywhere where the world cannot crowd in upon you. Close yourself in with the Lord. In His Presence, invite Him into your heart, your home, your life as Master.

Close your eyes to the things round about you. Listen for stillness. Relax your body. Breathe slowly and deeply as in sleep. Let go!

Let go of thoughts that torment you, thoughts of hurry and fear, of people and things. Think *up!* Think of infinite space, of endless time, of hushed silence—of God!

Open wide the door of your heart and accept love, just as a flower turns its face to the sun and accepts life. Say, softly and sincerely, "Come into my heart, Thou great Peace-giver. Flood me with tranquility." Let deep stillness fill your whole being. Cling to the image before your eyes— the image of One who loves you, who cares for you, who looks into the secret depths of your soul and recognizes your yearnings, longings, desires.

12

When old, disturbing thoughts threaten the calm that is beginning to enfold you, push them aside. Refuse to linger on them. Reach up again for the new thoughts. Take your Bible (have it near you always) and turn the pages to a throne scene, high and lifted up. From this vantage point you will get a new perspective; or turn to one of the Gospels and walk with Christ.

At the seaside hear Him speak peace to troubled hearts. Linger with Him at a well. Enter a boat and let the waves splash against it, while He speaks of the blessedness that awaits all who follow Him. Let Him whisper to *your* heart the words He once spoke to His disciples, "Peace I leave with you, my peace I give unto you: not as the world giveth, give I unto you. Let not your heart be troubled, neither let it be afraid (John 14:27. KJV). Yield in quiet acceptance. Let Him flood you with peace.

When you contrast your lovelessness and selfishness and pettiness to His love, your lips will pour out a confession of unworthiness, perhaps some special area of defeat. You will be released to tell Him all, as fully and honestly as you can. Bring Him your wounds to be healed, your sins to be forgiven, your work to be blessed, your troubled, restless heart to be stilled. He will be listening.

Tell Him you want your life to be guided by His Spirit; your problems solved by His wisdom; your weaknesses turned into strength by His help; your struggles turned into victories by His grace; your sorrows turned into joy by His comfort. In your imagination, watch Him take you by the hand to help you stand tall. Know that He has heard; He has forgiven you; He will sustain you.

Now, thank Him. Don't forget! You have received much; thank much.

Conversation is a two-way relationship. God listened to you speak. It is your turn to listen, as He speaks. It is an art to learn to hear Him speak. We hear with an inward receptivity, not with our physical ear. We know we have heard when some-

13

thing within us says, "This seems to be written just for me. This helps me." Each time you take the Bible in hand, read it with the thought that God has a message for you—He is trying to tell you something. When the message gets through to you, you will have heard. Let us assume that you are fearful and troubled. Read the twenty-third Psalm, "The Lord is my shepherd; I shall not want. . . ." When these words say to you, very personally, that God is your own protector, that He cares for you and will supply all your needs, then you will have heard. When your heart says, "Yes, I *ought* to thank Him, I ought to trust," you are hearing the still small voice of God. Pay close attention to the "I-ought-to" statements you make. You are putting into words the holy urges of God upon your heart.

Don't envy people whose lives seem more effective than yours. Remember, they got that way by coming into the light of Christ's Presence to listen to His voice. They went from His Presence aglow, ready to obey the instructions they received. You can do the same.

Thoughts to Make Your Day Glow

And this is life eternal, that they might know thee the only true God, and Jesus Christ whom thou hast sent (John 17:3, KJV).

God loves us, not for what we are, but for what He can make of us.

> When we look within we are depressed.
> When we look around we are impressed.
> When we look at Jesus we are blessed.

14

I want His imprint on my life.
He has claim to my life.
He gave it to me.

Very ordinary people, through friendship with Jesus become
extraordinary.

When once you have seen Jesus, you can never be the same.
Other things do not appeal as they used to.

2
BEING AVAILABLE TO GOD

When Moses faced the light of God's countenance on Mount
Sinai, his face shone with reflected glory. When we come into
the light of God's Presence something happens to us too.

One night, after I had spoken to a group about letting Christ
live *in* us so that He might enable us to live *for* Him, a young
man came up to me. The young man was in his twenties and,
although he was slow of speech, he was sincerely yielded to
Christ. "I know what you were talking about," he said. "I know
because it happened to me last week. I accepted Him as my personal Saviour and since then life is wonderful. Everything is

15

different, isn't it?" Then he looked questioningly at me and continued, "And you know what? Now, every morning, as soon as I awake I talk to my Lord. You know what I say to Him?"

"What?" I asked.

"I say, 'Good morning, Jesus. Thanks for today, and remember *I'm available!*' "

It was hard for me to hold back tears as I watched the light in his face. Simply—"I'm available." What complete commitment!

Some one once said to the young Dwight L. Moody, "It remains to be seen what God will do with a man who gives himself up wholly to Him." Moody said to himself, "I will be that man." And God accepted Moody's willingness and made of him a joyous personality, an instrument who brought thousands to the knowledge of Christ. God is just as ready to use you, if you are available. Won't you let the world see, today, what God can do with you because you are available to Him?

Once you make the big decision to belong to Him and to abandon your will to His direction, you must make a daily, even hourly, decision to yield every area of your life to Christ. Every lesser decision must be made on the same level of commitment. Then each day will be a step forward and upward in happy living.

As you awake each morning your first conscious thought should rise to the throne on high, in praise and thanksgiving for God's loving care during the night and for the light of a new day.

Your availability will help God to make it a good day for you, and a good one for His Kingdom. He will be able to send you where He needs you and to empower you to do what He wants you to do. Your whole day will be easier because the Presence will be with you.

Before you step out into the circle of your family and associates, pray again, "Lord, make me willing to be kind, understanding, and gracious. I am willing for your Spirit to flood my soul and control my every thought, emotion, and desire,

16

my every word and deed. Your Spirit's fruit is love, joy, peace, patience, kindness, goodness, faithfulness, gentleness, self-control. I need all of these in my life in order to live in harmony with my family and neighbors. Today, I am willing to smile at those who need a smile, to speak a cheery word to someone who is heavyhearted. You know who they are. Lead me to them." Your day will be radiantly happy. When you smile, others will smile back, and God will bless.

As you prepare to go to your place of employment remember that you may face stumbling blocks. An ungracious person may try your patience, or the monotony of the daily grind may get you down. Why not change these stumbling blocks into stepping stones? The word "willing" will do it. If you say to Him, "Lord, I am willing to love those who seem unlovely. I can't do it by myself. I have no love for them, but I am willing to accept an extra measure of Your love with which to love them." No chilly atmosphere will be able to rob you of peace, because the Spirit of peace will be within you. You will have grace to be Christlike in the most trying circumstances. Remember, there is no better place to show good manners than in the presence of bad manners. Prayer changes things. Prayer changes you.

Payday brings a tremendous challenge. When you are opening your pay envelope, try to pray, "Lord, I accept this from You. You are the Giver. I am willing to use this as You shall direct. If You so desire, I am willing to give my tithe, or more, to any work or person for whom You will burden me." The result will be beautiful experiences of guidance, joy in giving, and seeing the Kingdom progress because you have worked together with God. Instead of being irritated by requests to give, you will look for places to put your offering. God loves a cheerful giver. If you are *willing*, He will change you into one.

After work comes play. What you do with your leisure time can make or break you. Decisions need to be made as to the kind of friends, the kind of amusements, and places for amuse-

17

ment, your conduct, temptations, satisfactions. In the bewildering maze of influences that seek supremacy in the life of today's youth, how safe is he who can look up simply and ask, "Lord, do you approve?"

Anticipating a trip can be as stimulating as the trip itself. In planning your trip, do not leave God out of the plan. Wonderful things can happen if the traveler begins his journey with the prayer, "Lord, if there are any travelers on this bus or train or plane who need something You have given me, I am willing to share it. I am willing to sit with the person whom You choose, willing to be silent or to speak. I have neither wisdom nor tact nor courage to speak with others about spiritual matters, but I am available. Tell me what to say."

When He needs your service, God will open the way for you. And you will marvel at how easy it is—and how much fun!

As the church bells ring on Sunday morning and you enter the house of God, the spirit of willingness will help you make the hour sacred for you. Be willing to let God draw you unto Himself. Be willing to push the things of this world into the background. In your opening prayer, offer God the receptivity of your heart and mind. Be willing to let the Word of God chide you, cheer you, instruct you, strengthen you. In the holy sacrament, accept assurance of forgiveness and strength to mend your ways and to gain victory over your temptations thankfully. Do this with joy in remembrance of Him. Certain Greeks, who came to worship at the feast, were reported to have said, "Sir, we would see Jesus" (John 12:21, KJV). If that is your heart's hunger, you too shall find Him.

But, remember, there is also a time to report back. When day is done and gone the sun, come back once more to Jesus, as the disciples did. In Mark 6 we read that the apostles, when they were returned told Him all things both what they had done and what they had taught, and He said to them, "Come ye yourselves apart . . . and rest a while." Be sure that you, too, close each day, reporting back to your Master. Tell Him about your temptations, your successes and your defeats. Ask Him to forgive what was evil and to bless what was good in your life that day. Then pray, "Lord, even as I sleep, I am willing that your Spirit shall work in me. Convert my subconscious mind to willing obedience as you have converted my conscious mind to it. Then I shall not be full of tension, but I shall be able to sing, 'thanks be to God, which giveth us the victory through our Lord Jesus Christ'" (I Corinthians 15:57, KJV).

If you supply willingness, God will supply power. There is nothing too great; your willingness to let God work it out will reveal His mighty love and power.

Thoughts to Make Your Day Glow

. . . know the God of your father, and serve him with a whole heart and with a willing mind; for the Lord searches all hearts, and understands every plan and thought. If you seek him he will be found by you . . . (I Chronicles 28:9).

He leadeth me, O blessed thought! O words with heavenly
    comfort fraught!
Whate'er I do, where'er I be, Still 'tis God's hand that leadeth
    me.
He leadeth me, He leadeth me, By His own hand He leadeth me:
    His faithful follower I would be, For by His hand He
    leadeth me.

He Leadeth Me, JOSEPH H. GILMORE

Give me the power to live for mankind;
    Make me the mouth for such as cannot speak.

THEODORE PARKER

3
WATCHING THE CONTROL CENTER

As we think of the various facets of our lives that need to be watched, we must not bypass the control center—the tongue. The tongue is a major source of darkness or light in our lives. The Bible tells us that the tongue overflows what is in man's heart and mind. As we are inside, so will our speech be (Matthew 12:34–37; 15:18–19).

According to the dictionary, the tongue is simply a movable muscle used for tasting, eating and speaking. We know, however, because it is our instrument of communication, we equate it with all that is in our hearts and minds. And what a wonderful instrument of communication it is! By means of it, we can understand each other and the world in which we live.

When a television reporter announces that a world leader has died, the whole world knows it in minutes. If the tongue had not articulated this message over the air the world would have no knowledge of this event. The tongue is the master informer.

Freedom of speech is one of our greatest blessings. Think of nations where speech is silenced, where men whisper or avoid each other on the street for fear that what is on their minds may spill out and they will be turned over to a firing squad.

The tongue can be a wonderful vehicle of love. How handicapped we would be without the sweet words, "I love you." Even the tiny baby, cooing tender sounds, speaks to its mother of love. How poor the world would be if the Son of God had not spoken His words of love to us.

James tied together what we say with the quality of our religion: "Does anyone think he is a religious man? If he does not control his tongue his religion is worthless and he deceives himself. This is what God the Father considers to be pure and genuine religion: to take care of orphans and widows in their suffering, and to keep oneself from being corrupted by the world" (James 1:26–27 TEV).

In chapter 3 James delivers a classic essay on the tongue as fire:

> If anyone can control his tongue, it proves that he has perfect control over himself in every other way.
>
> We can make a large horse turn around and go wherever we want by means of a small bit in his mouth.
>
> And a tiny rudder makes a huge ship turn wherever the pilot wants it to go, even though the wind is strong.
>
> So also the tongue is a small thing, but what terrible results it can cause. A great forest can be set on fire by one tiny spark.
>
> And the tongue is a flame of fire. It is full of wickedness and poisons every part of the body. And the tongue is set on fire by hell itself, and can turn our whole lives into a blazing flame of destruction and disaster.
>
> Men have trained, or can train, every kind of animal or bird that lives and every kind of snake and fish,
>
> But no human being can tame the tongue. It is always ready to pour out its deadly poison.
>
> Sometimes it praises our heavenly Father, and sometimes it breaks out into curses against men who are made like God.
>
> And so blessing and cursing come pouring out of the same mouth. Dear brothers, surely this is not right (LIVING LETTERS).

When James says that the tongue is a fire, we need to ask what fire does. We know it has the power to blister, scorch and burn down to ashes. These words have become part of our daily vernacular. We say, "He gave a scorching message

21

against his opponent, a blistering accusation." Furthermore, we know that fire is hard to quench, that it starts up again easily, that it can leap and rage on. Any city fire department will testify to the truth of these words, so will your own heart. How difficult it is to quench bad feelings, to heal broken hearts that come from hot words. Fire is exciting. We all run to see where the fire is, when we see flames rising in the sky. Think of the excitement in gossip, especially if it is a very juicy bit of information. How exciting it is to repeat it. And so the evil of our tongues spreads. There is no divine law the tongue cannot break; it can cause a whole world of evil.

But you may say, "Yes, I agree, the tongue is as hard to control as a horse or a ship. I know from experience what trouble it can cause, but *how* can I control it? I have tried but I simply can't."

You are right; you cannot control your tongue simply by making up your mind that you will do so. Control comes from a deeper source—from your heart. When your heart is converted, your tongue will be converted. When your inner self is crucified, you can have a crucified tongue. When Christ's compassion and love overflow from your heart, your lips can speak loving words, forgiving words. You need to turn your helplessness over to Christ daily. Admit your lack of tongue control; confess it as sin and accept the help Christ offers, one day at a time. Don't be negative by repeating your helplessness. Be positive and thank Christ, that you may expect Him to change you. Then cooperate with Him. When impatient or ungracious words begin to arise, stop short. Refuse to say them. Change your tone of voice; relax your facial expression; look redeemed. The oftener you achieve this kind of victory the better you will be able to control your tongue. You and the world around you will be happier.

James tells us also that we can use our tongue to bless the Lord. What a contrast! What a privilege to tell of God's greatness. Throughout eternity we will want to use our tongues to thank and praise Him . . . world without end.

22

He who keeps his mouth and his tongue keeps himself out of trouble (Proverbs 21:23).

A fool gives full vent to his anger, but a wise man quietly holds it back (Proverbs 29:11).

It takes two or three years to learn to talk and the rest of your life to learn when not to talk.

If one is in the right, one need not lose one's temper; if one is in the wrong, one can't afford to lose it.

Words once spoken cannot be wiped out with a sponge.

4
ENJOYING COMMON THINGS

We are surrounded by loveliness, but in our daily haste often we pass them by. Awareness does not just happen. It needs to be pointed out how much being able to enjoy common things adds to life. As a young girl, an article that I read encouraged all of us to look for the beauty in ordinary things. The author said that if we started we would never stop, and we would always have something lovely to think about and speak about, and thus add beauty to our lives.

I hope the reading of this page will do that for you.

In my earliest childhood, my good father taught me to see the beauty in common clover blossoms. I spent the first nine years of my life in a country parsonage where clover grew in abundance. It lined both sides of the country road which led to our school, a quarter of a mile away. The early morning walks to school, when the earth was bathed in night's coolness and dew, were unforgettable. The fragrance of plowed soil or new-mown hay rose pungent and pure into our nostrils. A holy stillness surrounded us, broken only by the song of a thrush. Little gophers sat up and looked at us, then scampered across the road. Even now, in a big apartment house in a big city, it is refreshing to pause and relive the awe and wonder of those days—the sweet security of walking with a dear father and waiting, as he picked a clover blossom to show to me.

Each year, the girls in school waged a contest to see who could find the most four-leaf clovers. Years of looking for them so trained my eyes, that even today, all I have to do is stoop and pick them—they seem to jump up at me. A four-leaf clover pressed in a book, and suddenly rediscovered, brings back wonderful memories.

A bouquet of clover and wild grasses on my desk speaks worlds to me. I don't need hothouse roses, lovely as they are —a clover blossom says enough!

This summer, a young woman came to me all excited about a discovery she had made about a nearby catalpa tree. Although its large, heart-shaped leaves and huge flowers have been there for years, it was perhaps, the least admired of trees. People usually said, "It grows fast, but it's so messy when the flowers and long beans drop."

24

This day, for the first time, the young woman was attracted by the display of blossoms. She picked a cluster and paused to examine it. To her amazement she beheld a cone-shaped arrangement of many exquisite orchids, each one a world of beauty. Her joy was unbounded—her special joy for that day. Never pass a catalpa tree in bloom without taking the time to behold the Creator's exquisite handiwork!

Seeing a bird's nest on the branch of a tree is a delight to all of us, especially to little boys. Curiosity leads them to dangerous heights. They must climb to see what is in the nest. They must peek to satisfy their desire to see the unusual and rightly so.

When they run to show us what they have found, it is important to teach them respect for what is most precious to the mother bird—its nest and its young—to teach them not to touch or rob the nest. Better still, teach them before they start climbing trees.

There is a very lovely verse, taught to young children in another language, in which a mother speaks:

> Little boy, I plead with you as earnestly as I can.
> Oh, don't touch my little nest.
> Please don't look into it with your glances,
> Because you see, my babies are lying therein.
> They will be terrified and scream with fright
> If you look at them with your great big eyes.

Let's begin to teach very little children—and let's keep on with older ones—respect for everything that has life. Let's help them become aware of the beauty and wonder all around them.

Never lose an opportunity to look on a beautiful thing, for it will leave a touch of new beauty in your life. Looking upon Jesus will print new glory in your soul.

25

Thoughts to Make Your Day Glow

God of the hills, grant me Thy strength to go back into the cities without faltering; strength to do my daily task without tiring and with enthusiasm; strength to help my neighbor who has no hills to remember.

God of the lake, grant me Thy peace and Thy restfulness; peace to bring into the world of hurry and confusion; restfulness to carry to the tired one whom I shall meet every day; content to do small things with freedom from littleness; self-control for the unexpected emergency and patience for the wearisome task, with a deep depth within my soul, to bear with me through crowded places the hush of the nighttime when the pine trees are dark against the skyline; the humbleness of the hills who in their mightiness know it not; the laughter of the sunny days to brighten the cheerless spots in the long winter.

God of the stars, may I take the gift of friendship and love for all. Fill me with a tenderness for the needy person at every turning.

Prayer of a Camper, AUTHOR UNKNOWN

THE CAMP HYMN

God, who touchest earth with beauty,
Make my heart anew;
With thy Spirit re-create me,
Pure, and strong, and true.

Like thy springs and running waters,
Make me crystal pure;
Like the rocks of towering grandeur,
Make me strong and sure.

Like thy dancing waves in sunlight,
Make me glad and free;
Like the straightness of the pine trees
Let me upright be.

Like the arching of the heavens
Lift my thoughts above,
Turn my dreams to noble action—
Ministries of love.

God, who touchest earth with beauty,
Make my heart anew;
Keep me ever by thy spirit,
Pure, and strong, and true.   Amen.

MARY S. EDGAR

5
ENJOYING UNCOMMON THINGS

Understanding and appreciating people and things of other cultures can add much joy to our lives. It can be a great step toward building peace and goodwill among men, also.

I was shocked to have a United States serviceman, who had

returned from a tour of duty in Europe tell me, "I didn't like the people of that country. They were so old-fashioned. When I was on leave, I stayed in the barracks and read. Those people didn't interest me and I didn't like their language." When I got over my surprise, I asked myself, "How did we fail this young man? Had no one ever opened his eyes to new and different things? To understand the culture and history of other lands?" He came back smaller in heart and mind, when he could have broadened his horizon.

On one of my visits to Europe, a number of years ago, I had one of the most delightful experiences of my life. We had gone out into the coffee corner of the garden, surrounded by lovely bushes and trees, to enjoy our breakfast. Suddenly, we heard a noise. It sounded like someone clapping two boards of wood together very hard and fast. Again we heard it. Finally, our eyes were drawn to the thatched roof of a two-hundred-and-fifty-year-old parsonage, where three storks were perched on a nest. Questions flew and this is the story we were told.

Decades ago someone placed a wagon wheel flat on the housetop in order to provide a landing platform and a firm foundation for a stork nest. The nest (called a *horst*) grows taller each year because the storks put a new floor on top of the old one before they set up housekeeping, in the spring. From where we sat the *horst* seemed to be about five feet tall. Each year a stork and his new wife come to this housetop nest. In April, the local people begin to talk about their stork and to wonder if he will be back. Because a stork can live to be seventy years old and because he always returns to his same nest, the local people speak of "our stork." Each year the storks come back at the same time, between the fourth and sixth day of April and they always leave again on August twenty-second.

There is room only for father, mother and one child in the nest. If more than one egg hatches, the excess member of

28

eir hearts to let us know their secrets of the over-
By means of words, our lives, too, are broadened
ore fully.

n who can enjoy words and their origins is for-
d. How rewarding it is to look up the meaning
iliar word, or even a familiar one, and to trace
om a basic language.

er the day I discovered how the word *sanctification*
gether: *sanctus* meaning "holy," *ification* meaning
the process of being made holy.

eeded to know what the word "holy" really means
that it means to be separated from the world and
unto God. Thus, to sanctify any place, day, sea-
on means to declare that it belongs to God. Sanctified
worship are the church building, the altar, the

t does the word "worship" really mean? Its origin is
tion of the two Anglo-Saxon words "worth" and
d it means religious reverence.

rd "religion" comes from two Latin words, *re* mean-
," and *ligare* meaning to "bind;" in other words,
f man to a higher power.

vages, wandering in forests, felt a power in the
orld about them that they did not understand. To
ry phenomenon they could not understand was a spirit:
ackling stick, lightning, thunder, wind, the howling
were spirits, which could harm them. They thought
ge taboos, magic formulas and human sacrifices in
bribe these spirits to be friendly. They called what
and what they did *religo*, meaning "to bind fast."

on represents man's desire and effort to bind him-
and secure to the great Spirit of the universe. We see
herent longing for God the Creator, the need to belong

hould thank God that we need not seek restlessly for

the family is thrown overboard. In the winter the storks fly to Northern Africa, but in the spring they return to European communities that have little streams and swamps nearby which supply food such as frogs and snakes.

We saw one stork family, each standing on only one leg, on the roof of a men's clothing store right downtown in a small city. There we were told that every year since 1850, without exception, storks have used this *horst*.

Preparation for the flight to Africa is interesting for the people to watch. Days before August twenty-second, the birds practice wingspread and violent flapping. As the date for departure approaches, larger groups of storks fly overhead, barely visible. Finally, the gathering of all takes place in a meadow as if to plan travel strategy. Comes the twenty-second and away they all fly.

No doubt, you are asking as we did, "How do they know dates? How do they know the way to faraway lands in Africa? How do they know the art of nest building?" Instinct, we say. But who gave them this instinct? Jeremiah, the prophet, was instructed to appeal to God's estranged people with these words of God: ". . . Amend your ways and your doings. . . . Why then has this people turned away in perpetual backsliding. . . . Even the stork in the heavens knows her times; and the turtledove, swallow, and crane keep the time of their coming but my people know not the ordinances of the Lord" (Jeremiah 7:3; 8:5, 7).

How rich this day was for us—what an exhibit of another one of God's lovelinesses!

Thinking of wingspread, I am reminded of other feathered friends, which the Bible mentions. What better picture of security could God have given us than the protection of eagle wings! (Exodus 19:4)

But we need not travel abroad to see uncommon things, we can find them in our own country right in my native state of Nebraska. My father used to tell of three strange and unlikely animals, which according to folklore lived in the same hole in the ground—the prairie dog, the rattlesnake and the owl. In checking the authenticity of this phenomenon recently, I found that it is true—all three can be seen in the same area. Prairie dogs live in "towns" that may cover several acres. As the population of these towns does not remain static, there are many abandoned burrows. Rather than dig their own holes, the rattlesnakes and owls move into the abandoned prairie dog tunnels. Towns are usually located on the flat, and mounds are piled around the entrances. Snakes are fond of sunning themselves and these mounds work out very well for this purpose. So, the owl, the snake and the prairie dog share the same burrows. Good inter-animal relations!

What other things are there for you to discover and enjoy, perhaps right in your own back yard? Oh, to have open eyes and a heart to praise our Creator.

Read with me Chapters 38–39 in Job in which the Lord tells of the creatures which, in His great wisdom, He made. Read the story of His snow, hail, lightning; the sea, springs and clouds; the ostrich, hawk, eagle, horse, hippopotamus, crocodile. This rehearsal was to prove to Job that God is all-wise and that He makes no mistakes. Overwhelmed, Job cries out, "I know that thou canst do all things, and that no purpose of thine can be thwarted" (42:2).

Thoughts to Make Your Day Glow

Thus says the Lord, the Holy one of Israel. . . . Will you . . . command me concerning the work of my hands? I made the earth, and created man upon it (Isaiah 45:11–12).

30

The earth is the L
those who dwell the

Blessed be his glori
whole earth! Amen

Praise to the Lord, w
Shieldeth thee under
   Hast thou not see
   How thy desires e
Granted in what he ord

SEEING THE V

Words have a strange pow
laughter or tears, to serious c
to courage and action. Words
memories. Great truths are cor

By means of words, our Lor
the gospel. By means of words

31

Him, that He has sought us in His love, and that we are secure in His Presence. We need to preach this message here in our land, and we need to bring it to tribes and nations, which still seek to bind themselves to an unknown god. They need our "wonderful words of love."

The importance of words is evident in the works of missionaries and the Bible translators, who go before them or who work with them. Think of a Bible translator living with an illiterate tribe for months before he can find a word in their language to express the concept of fear or worry. Think of his joy when he hears the old chief say, "I shiver in my liver." The very words the translator was looking for! How would you and I like to explain to a desert dweller what Noah's ark was? But words *were* found, words that proved adequate— "huge water box." For the word "hypocrite" the natives said, "man with two hearts"; for "church," "praise-God-house"; for "worship," "wag your tail before God"; to "kiss," "greet by smelling faces"; "to die," "to pass out through the big toe." Oh, the wonder of words! They can add so much to our lives!

The Bible tells us the origin of the names of everything God created in the animal world. After God had formed the earth, the sun, moon and stars, all birds, fish, and cattle, He made man. Knowing that it was not good that man should be alone, God had all animals pass before Adam so he could name each one. "God . . . brought them to the man to see what he would call them; and whatever the man called every living creature, that was its name" (Genesis 2:19). Man, in his original purity and wisdom, was able to choose names for all cattle, birds, and every beast of the field.

Interesting, too, is what follows this account. Having seen and named all creatures, Adam found not one that was fit to be a companion to him. It was then that God made a helper fit for him—woman.

Haven't you ever wondered how so many delightful idioms

33

came into popular usage? The source of many of our expressions is the Bible. You are using Biblical wordage when you speak of: "a drop in the bucket," "at wit's end," "give up the ghost," "the root of the matter," "see eye to eye," "the apple of your eye," "a man after my own heart," "a good old age."

Words can be like a refreshing drink. A friend, describing a storm which had raged all night, roaring and bending trees low by its might, said, "Wasn't it majestic? It seemed to me I heard the trees clapping their hands for joy." Isn't that expressive? It made me think of Psalm 98:7-8, "Let the sea roar, and all that fills it; the world and those who dwell in it! Let the floods clap their hands; let the hills sing for joy together."

And of Isaiah 55:12, "For you shall go out in joy, and be led forth in peace; the mountains and the hills before you shall break forth into singing, and all the trees of the field shall clap their hands."

Let us understand, also, that the language to which we were born has power to reach into the soul, because we learned these words at our mother's knees in her own language. The words still speak to our hearts. I was reared in a bilingual home and I can still remember the first time I prayed the Lord's prayer in English. I felt that I was speaking to a stranger, because until then I had always addressed God in my mother's tongue.

Doesn't the wonder of words make you wonder, with me, what celestial words we will have at our command when we shall come into the presence of the cherubim and seraphim who give glory to the Lamb upon the Throne, and whom we are to join in the everlasting praise, world without end?

Thoughts to Make Your Day Glow

Heaven and earth will pass away, but my words will not pass away (Matthew 24:35).

". . . but the word of the Lord abides forever." That word is the good news which was preached to you (I Peter 1:25).

Good sayings are like pearls strung together.

I like not only to be loved, but to be told that I am loved. . . . the realm of silence is large enough beyond the grave.

GEORGE ELIOT

7
EXPLORING NEW INSIGHTS

Luke's account of the life of Christ gives us the delightful event of Easter afternoon. "Two of them" (Were they husband and wife or friends?) walked the seven miles from Jerusalem to Emmaus. Jesus, catching up with them, joined in their conversation. When they arrived at their destination, Jesus was invited to abide with them. And, while He offered the table prayer, *their eyes were opened*, and He vanished. Later that evening, when those same two and the eleven were gathered together, suddenly Jesus stood among them to bring peace to their troubled hearts. Then He *opened their minds* to understand. The new insight they gained, after their minds were opened, revolutionized their whole lives. "He is alive. He is risen indeed" now explained everything else. It was so important to them that they devoted the rest of their lives to the telling of it.

In our Christian growth, our eyes and minds must be opened to new insights, also. Words, phrases, teachings, which are devoid of meaning to us today, must with spiritual maturing become clearer to us. What joy to experience the unfolding of a truth which had escaped us earlier. Even little shades of meaning or application of them brighten the pages, and our days.

One student wrote, in the margins of her Bible, the date and the name of the one who helped her to see new meaning in the verses. This act perpetuated her joy of discovery every time she saw those pages.

Recently I gained additional meaning for the word "fruit." I have, of course, known the word "fruit" since I was a child —apples, pears, cherries. But in His farewell instructions to His disciples, our Lord said, ". . . I chose you and appointed you that you should go and bear fruit and that your fruit should abide . . ." (John 15:16). Previously, He had said, "You are the salt of the earth. . . . You are the light of the world . . ." (Matthew 5:13, 14). Men were to *see* good works in his disciples. They were to see qualities like love, patience, kindness, forgiveness, self-control. Seeing these fruits would convince them. We might also add that the fruits of the disciples' labor were the souls won for Christ.

A third concept that has come to me: fruit is not only to be seen and admired, its real purpose is to nourish those who use it for food. After I see a beautiful apple on a tree and admire it, I am to eat it and be strengthened by it.

I ask, "Are others nourished by anything they receive from my life?" When Paul was in prison, his daily conduct and witness were such ripe fruits that his fearful friends became "much more bold to speak the word of God without fear" (Philippians 1:14). Not only did they *see* Paul's courage in the face of torture and death, they *fed* on it and became strong to face their own threats.

The source of fruit bearing is Christ Himself, ". . . filled with the fruits of righteousness which come through Jesus Christ . . ." (Philippians 1:11). He is the vine and we the branches. His "sap," His Spirit, flowing through us ripens us for fruit bearing.

We never know where or when we will receive these new insights. We must ever be on the lookout for them, as we read, as we listen, as we meditate. The beginning of a meditation on a church bulletin caught my attention: "I wish He had not said it." It continued, "He who has two coats, let him share with him who has none. I have more than two coats, several old ones hanging unused in a closet. The trouble is that almost everyone I know has more than two coats also. Where will I find a man without a coat at all? I wish He had not said it, simply because I have a suspicion that He was talking about something more than coats. . . ."

Before I read this meditation I had limited my understanding of two coats to clothing. If some one needed clothing, I should be willing to give some of mine away; if groups of destitute people, like those in refugee camps, needed clothing I should give.

Now, I took a second look at the words, "two coats." Could Christ have been talking about something more than clothing? Was he, perhaps, giving us a principle of sharing, using two coats to illustrate what He meant? What else do we have to

37

give? I have friends. Could it be that I am to give my friendship to the friendless person—my second coat?

I have concerned loved ones who care about my welfare and
happiness. Could it be that Christ wants me to give my concern
to those who have no one who cares—my second coat?

I have many hours each day for my own interests. Could it
be that I am to give some of my time for lonely souls, for
worthy causes—my second coat?

I have dollars and cents at my disposal. Could it be that I
am to give some to those who are in want—my second coat?

I am richer for the new insight!

Thoughts to Make Your Day Glow

Love is like sunlight which ripens fruit.

What I am is God's gift to me;
    What I do with it is my gift to Him.

If we belong to God, we also belong to one another.

II
Every Moment of Life

8
LIFE, GOD'S GIFT

Many years ago, I read these words of a well-known poem: "Only one life, t'will soon be past." They spoke powerfully to my heart, urging me to make the most of my one and only life. Only once am I privileged to be among the living, to walk across life's stage. There is an entrance and an exit and, in between, I am to live out my few short years minute by minute.

Realization that life is a gift from God is the beginning of effective living. I accept this gift from the Giver with thanks, and I guard it as a precious treasure.

When I was very young, someone said to me, "Next Friday will be your birthday." I wanted it to be Friday right away. Then a deep insight came to me, small as I was, that Friday would come only as I went through each day and each night, each hour and each minute toward Friday.

Another vivid realization came to me later in life, in a strange way. I was attending a chapel service at school. The invited speaker rose to read a text. His first words were, "I wish I were a cat." What poor taste, I thought, tensing up and wondering what cats had to do with the text. The speaker did have my attention, however, and after fifteen years I still remember the lesson. "I wish I had nine lives as the cat prover-

bially has." That was his point. "There is so much I want
to do and learn and explore and enjoy that one life will not be
enough." I agreed and relaxed. Then he went on, "If I had nine
lives, then each single one would not be so all-important. I
could afford to use one for travel, another one to satisfy my
musical interest, another one to make money." I'll never forget
the long pause and the quiet musing before he went on, "But
I don't have nine lives. I have only one, and much of that one
is gone. I guess I'll just have to make the most of what is left
of this one."

Thoughts to Make Your Day Glow

The only way to live is by accepting each moment as an unre-
peatable miracle.

Every man also to whom God has given wealth and possessions
and power to enjoy them, and to accept his lot and find enjoy-
ment in his toil—this is the gift of God (Ecclesiastes 5:19).

I have seen the business that God has given to the sons of men
to be busy with. He has made everything beautiful in its time;
also he has put eternity into man's mind. . . . I know that
there is nothing better for them than to be happy and enjoy
themselves as long as they live; also that it is God's gift to man
that every one should eat and drink and take pleasure in all
his toil (Ecclesiastes 3:10, 12–13).

42

9
LIFE IN SMALL DOSES

Life is lived at its best when taken in small doses. For that reason it was given us in daily rations. Jesus said, "Therefore do not be anxious about tomorrow. . . . Let the day's own trouble be sufficient for the day" (Matthew 6:34). We would panic if we had to think of being good and doing what is right for possibly eighty years. God has graciously divided the years into months, the months into weeks, the weeks into days, the days into hours, minutes and seconds, so that we can handle life's responsibilities as they come to us. The question is not, "Can I make a success of my total life?" but "Is God able to keep me and lead me safely one day at a time, one step at a time, one decision at a time, one crisis at a time?"

The psalmist showed me how he did it, "Seven times a day I praise thee for thy righteous ordinances;

Great peace have those who love thy law; nothing can make them stumble" (119:164–165).

Thoughts to Make Your Day Glow

Those who have learned the art of abiding under pressure
are those who are able to go through life without
breaking under the strain.

The burdens of life are only for each day as it comes.

Life by the inch is a cinch,
    Life by the yard is hard!

43

10
LIFE WITH A PURPOSE

I want to live each day in the glow of a divine purpose. Someone once said, "I live each day urged on by my one purpose for existence. The quality of my life depends upon how exalted my purpose for living is. I have deliberately chosen a chief aim for my life. Not until I actually asked myself, 'Why am I here?' and worked out my own answer did I live with a purpose."

Multitudes seem to live without a purpose, but they too have one, even if it is only to live for self-indulgence.

Some time ago, I learned of a bachelor who came to an attorney to have his last will drawn up. "I'm getting old," he said, "and I suppose I should make some plan to dispose of my possessions. I have worked very hard all my life. I have saved and never allowed myself anything for pleasure. I worked hard to pay for my farm. When that was debt-free, I bought a second farm and worked hard and saved. Then I bought a third farm and did the same thing over again. Now, after all this hard work, what shall I do with the three farms? They are on my hands and I don't know why I worked like crazy to get them. I have no children and no near relatives. What shall I do? I have thought of giving them to the state. . . ."

The lawyer interrupted him, "wait a minute before you do that. Did you ever think of giving anything to others to make them happy?"

"No, I never have. All I thought of was to keep."

"Did you ever give to the church?"

"No, I saved that money."

"Did you ever give to community agencies that help people in need?"

"No, I had to pay for the farms."

Unfortunately, the lawyer was not able to show the bachelor, that in the short span of life he had left, he could do much with his possessions to bring happiness to others and to himself. His life pattern was hardened—set. He was a slave in a prison he had made himself.

This is, of course, the extreme example of a misspent life, but many of us also miss the mark in varying degrees. Check your life purpose with the one given in the Scriptures—believe in Christ and go out to practice love (I John 3:23). His love, flowing into our hearts, is to overflow in service to others. Let us remember that the older we grow the less flexible our life patterns become. Check right now. Are you living for the highest purpose?

Thoughts to Make Your Day Glow

Wealth is not his that has it, but his that enjoys it.

Money is a good servant, but a dangerous master.

In the hum of the market there is money, but under the cherry tree there is rest.

11
MAN'S BRIEF EXISTENCE

To make the most of this one life one must be aware of the brevity of human existence and of God's timelessness. As the days and years slip away, I must ever be aware that I shall not be here forever. This thought is not a morbid one, but a happy thanking of God each new morning for another day in which to live and serve, knowing that one day I shall be called home. The word *home* helps us.

The Bible says, "Man that is born of a woman is of few days, and full of trouble. He comes forth like a flower, and withers; he flees like a shadow, and continues not" (Job 14: 1–2). We are aware that sooner or later the call will come, "Time's up. Return." And this is very final! In the meantime, we want to make the most of the fragile gift of *time*. I saw, on a bulletin board somewhere, "Life is fragile. Handle with prayer." In the end we must give an account of how we spent the time He gave us. There is a day of reckoning coming. Then, our lives will be weighed to see if they had enough content. "Self" weighs very light. "Service" weighs heavier. "Honoring God" weighs heaviest.

In the book of Daniel we read the powerful drama of a man being weighed in his zero hour. Belshazzar, the king of Chaldea made a great feast and invited a thousand of his lords. As they feasted and drank, the fingers of a man's hand appeared and wrote on the plaster of the wall. The king saw it and was alarmed. He called for enchanters and astrologers to explain the meaning of this uncanny handwriting. When they could not, Daniel, a handsome young exile from Judah was brought in, and he interpreted the handwriting: ". . . you . . . have not humbled your heart . . . but you have lifted up yourself against the Lord of heaven . . . but the God in whose hand is your

breath, and whose are all your ways, you have not honored.
. . . God has numbered the days of your kingdom and brought
it to an end; . . . you have been weighed in the balances and
found wanting; . . . your kingdom is divided and given to the
Medes and Persians" (5:22–23; 26–28).
That very night Belshazzar was slain and his kingdom given
to others.

This account has much to say to us. True, it happened some
6,000 years B.C. but, just as Belshazzar lived for self and for
pleasure and did not honor God, so we are warned lest in a
measure we do likewise. We are to learn that selfish, worldly
living finally weighs too light. "Every way of a man is right
in his own eyes, but the Lord weighs the heart" (Proverbs
21:2).

Solomon, the writer of Ecclesiastes, gives an interesting account of how he evaluated his life efforts and accomplish-
ments in light of life's shortness. He records his human thoughts
against God's thoughts and gives us an insight into his search
for a life goal, when he was out of fellowship with his God.
First, he wondered how he could find satisfaction and happiness
apart from God: "Vanity of vanities! All is vanity. What does
man gain by all the toil at which he toils under the sun?"
(1:2–3). It all seemed futile, worthless, empty, fruitless, valueless. Then he sought satisfaction from science, but could get no
answer. He sought vainly to find it in philosophy, in pleasure,
mirth, drinking, building, possessions, wealth and music—all
were empty! Even morality proved fruitless to him. Finally,
after having tried all self-effort at finding meaning to life,
he concluded with this clear statement of real worth, "The
end of the matter; all has been heard. Fear God, and keep his
commandments; for this is the whole duty of man. For God will
bring every deed into judgment, with every secret thing, whether
good or evil" (12:13).

Letting the Lord live in us, and following His directions
leads to meaningful living—life with weighty content.

Thoughts to Make Your Day Glow

Lord, through all the generations You have been our home! Before the mountains were created, before the earth was formed, You are God without beginning or end.

You speak, and man turns back to dust.

A thousand years are but as yesterday to You! They are like a single hour!

. . . Seventy years are given us! And some may even live to 80. But even the best of these years are often emptiness and pain; soon they disappear, and we are gone.

. . . Teach us to number our days and recognize how few they are; help us to spend them as we should . . . (Psalm 90, LIVING PSALMS).

Wish not so much to live long, as to live well.

He who does good is of God . . . (III John 11).

12
EACH DAY'S EXTRA JOYS

I sent a greeting to a friend I had not seen in years, and in his reply, he wrote, "Every day has some extra joy, and the day I received your letter was God's offering for that day." This one sentence unlocked the secret of his triumphant life. It was filled with happy achievement in spite of a severe handicap. Every day he expected some extra joy and every day it was there.

Since I received his letter, each evening I have actually kept track to see if there really was something special about that day. And sure enough, each night I could give thanks for a special joy, as I went to rest. Each morning, I could give thanks again for what was yet to come in the new day.

If we keep an eye open for the plusses that brighten our days, we can do as the psalmist did—praise God seven times a day, yea, more than seven times.

Thoughts to Make Your Day Glow

This is the day which the Lord has made; let us rejoice and be glad in it (Psalm 118:24).

An extra day is time for extra happiness!

This day is very special; different from yesterday, different from tomorrow. It is here. In it I live!

And every day I will say, "There's something happy on the way, and God sends love to me."

13
GOOD DAYS

To enjoy the greatest possible measure of health I need to avoid those things which war against the constant revitalizing, refreshing, renewing power built into me.

God uses the natural and near-at-hand forces to keep me strong—fresh air, sunshine, food and medicine. But, along with balanced diet, adequate rest and exercise there is one more important ingredient—a cheerful heart!

I dare not give in to self-pity, anger, worry, guilt. These will tear down my resistance to infection. I can get rid of these one day at a time, as I come into the Presence of Him who forgives, who releases, who restores (preferably in the morning). In all honesty of heart, I can come, admitting my areas of tension, asking for forgiveness and accepting His help. Then, I can go on my way fortified.

A good way to begin the morning is to sit completely still for a few moments, eyes closed until you are physically relaxed, to think up to the Source of every good thing. I suggest that you experiment using the verb "I accept." It dramatizes what faith means. Pray, "Lord, I accept right now the forgiveness of all my sin. I accept Your peace; let it flow over me and into my very being. I accept Your healing power. Where there is infection in my body I accept the touch of Your finger of healing. Burn out the sick cells and increase the normal, well cells. I accept for this day a happy outlook. Make me too happy to complain, too concerned about the happiness of others to concentrate on self. Let me seek beauty and find it in nature, in color, in music, in literature, in people. Let me speak only that which will help others to have a cheerful heart. I accept every strength I will need for this day. And, Lord, grant me one more favor—help me to accept it all with overflowing thanks."

Now, act as if God is at work within you because you are God's child!

Thoughts to Make Your Day Glow

A cheerful heart is a good medicine, but a downcast spirit dries up the bones (Proverbs 17:22).

A man's spirit will endure sickness; but a broken spirit who can bear? (Proverbs 18:14).

The best physicians are Dr. Diet, Dr. Quiet and Dr. Merryman.

Cheerfulness builds health.
   Health builds cheerfulness.

14
BAD NIGHTS

In every human life, difficult days will bring sorrow and disappointment. During such days, God is eager to use the opportunity to whisper great truths into our ears. Often, we are too preoccupied during the day to listen to Him, so He must use the stillness of the night to make Himself heard. It may take a special course in the school of suffering for us to pay attention to what is most important for our eternal well-being. God does not *send* troubles to us. (We bring many of them on ourselves by disobeying His laws of safety, health and love.) But he does *permit* them to come to us, and He will use them for our good, if we are willing to listen to Him.

All day long your mind is crowded with a multitude of influences, conversations, letters, programs and slogans, each one adding to the complexity of your life. When evening comes you hope to choose your own thoughts. Before the day closes perhaps you also think of God, sharing with Him what troubled you and what rejoiced your heart. Then you lay your head on the pillow and seek rest. The day is completed.

Rest comes, but, alas, does not last through the night. Before long, you find yourself awake. You begin to fear that you will not be fresh and alert for the duties of the next day. As sleeplessness continues, you get tense. You toss and turn and dig into your pillow. But the worst part of the ordeal is that annoying thoughts persist in returning again and again, each one in turn enlarging the worry.

Yes, we all know about such sleepless nights, but what we do not know is that they need not be so torturous. If you doubt that such nights can become a blessing, let me tell you how.

When you first awake in the wee hours of the night, say to

yourself "This will not hurt me. There is nothing serious about being awake for a while. I may not sleep, but my body can rest, and the healing, restoring processes need not be interrupted. I will relax and expect to arise refreshed. I will refuse to linger on disturbing thoughts and will substitute thanksgiving for every remembered good that has come to me. I will dream of ways I can bring happiness to others."

As your thoughts move from topic to topic you will be able to see definite solutions to problems, gain new values and enlarged viewpoints. Sleep will return and morning will come. You will arise enlightened, encouraged, directed.

Longer periods of being shut in can be rich also, with the possibility of an adventure into great and secret things. Between periods of pain and drowsiness, moments come in which the soul reaches up for something beyond the commonplace —to something eternal.

If that hunger is awake in you now, you will be cheered to read the words the Lord spoke to the prophet Jeremiah when he was shut in, "Call to me and I will answer you, and will tell you great and hidden things which you have not known" (33:3). These words are meant for you also. Claim them. Individuals who are not seasoned and ripened in adversity may think my reasoning strange. To them, we say, "It means abiding in Christ, trusting Him so completely that struggle ceases more and more. Alone, this cannot be accomplished. We need the help of the Holy Spirit. Through the Word we need to be assured that God makes no mistakes, and that what He permits to come to us, He will use for our good, unpleasant as it may seem for the moment."

It would be well to read the four gospels again, to find out what instructions our Lord gave on how to pray prayers which He can answer. We should memorize the wonderful promises of answers to prayer. With these, we can meet doubts as they arise. Learn, for instance this affirmation of faith, "and this is the confidence which we have in him, that if we ask anything according to his will, he hears us. And if we know that he hears us in whatever we ask, we know that we have obtained the requests made of him" (I John 5:14–15).

Perhaps you have called and you seem to be getting no answer. What have you called for? Only to be delivered from your trouble? There is a great secret you need to learn: anything that drives you closer to your Lord and deeper into the search for truth will work for your good. Therefore, your greatest happiness just now, may not lie in release from pain and trouble but in dependence upon divine strength.

It may seem strange to pray for anything but quick and complete release from suffering and trouble. But, if you are to learn the secret of your greatest good, your prayer may need to be, "Lord, teach me to pray the kind of prayers You can answer. I do not know what is best for me. Make me willing to accept whatever comes from Your hand. Tomorrow I shall come back for tomorrow's help. Give me a real sense of Your nearness, and if You are trying to say something special to me, I will listen. In the meantime make me into the kind of person whom You can use."

After the Lord, through Jeremiah, said, "Call to me," He also said, "I will answer you." That statement is definite and final. We can rest assured that God means what He says. We can have faith in His faithfulness. The trouble lies not in His willingness to answer but in our inability to hear and understand the answer sent. We need to open all the doors of our inner life in receptivity.

What makes us dull of hearing? A number of barriers which we ourselves set up, perhaps without realizing it.

A hurried, restless heart is never in tune to catch divine messages. Only in periods of quiet can we hear the still, small voice.

Guilt and fear, like two monsters, rise up against us to disturb our hearts and minds unless we flee to God for refuge.

Lack of knowledge, especially of what God is like, robs us

54

of freedom to approach Him as children come to their loving fathers—in trust. Not knowing glorious promises of help and guidance prevents us from using them as foundations upon which to stand firm and unafraid.

Vagueness in praying prevents us from asking for specific blessings, and from expecting to receive them. Having them, we fail to recognize them and to give thanks for them.

An unwilling spirit, which rebels at God's way, closes completely the ear of faith and opens the heart to bitterness and doubt.

Remember, God would often be unjust if He answered all of our prayers and requests. The psalmist humbly said to his God, "I know, O Lord, that thy judgments are right, and that in faithfulness thou hast afflicted me" (119:75).

Thoughts to Make Your Day Glow

Christians, like tea, grow strong when they are in hot water!

If man could have half his wishes, he would double his troubles.

All sunshine makes the desert!

ARAB PROVERB

Sometimes we need to wash out our eyes with tears so that we can better see Christ.

A gem is not polished without rubbing, nor a man perfected without trials.

55

15
DAYS OF FESTIVITY

Thanksgiving Day

Each year you and I join in national giving of thanks. For a nation to give thanks is not new, and it certainly is not limited to our American Thanksgiving Day.

The first pages of Hebrew Scriptures tell the story of Adam. After we are told of Adam's sons and their descendents, the account closes with this statement: ". . . then began men to call upon the name of the Lord" (Genesis 4:26b, KJV). How long ago was that? Possibly some six thousand years ago? At that time, men began to call upon the name of the Lord which, most likely, means that they began to worship Jehovah by public prayer and sacrifice.

The prayer, no doubt, included thanks for God's goodness in supplying rains and growth so that men could eat. The sacrifice was a religious act in which an offering—a material object like grain, fruit or sheep—was made to God. This offering was laid on an altar and consumed by fire. The purpose was to dramatize men's desire to get right with God through forgiveness, to enjoy again a friendly relationship with God. It expressed faith in God, repentance for man's failures, and adoration for God Himself, His justice and love. God accepted man's sacrifice and thanks and restored the broken relationship.

Later, God Himself instructed His people to observe feasts, as a teaching device, to keep alive faith in Him and to encourage His people to remember Him regularly, in a special way. There were eight such feasts: Sabbath, Passover, Pentecost, Trumpets, Atonement, Tabernacles, the Sabbath year and the

Jubilee. This meant that the people celebrated the nearness and goodness of their God constantly.

It is interesting that in our Thanksgiving Day observance we have combined both emphases—the public thanks service, in which we express our gratitude in corporate assembly, and our family feasts in which we seek to dramatize the abundance of God's provision by feasting on what he caused to grow and ripen. Although centuries have passed we have not deviated much from the old pattern. Man still feels the necessity to thank Someone and to rejoice with his fellow man. Pity the unbelievers who, overflowing with gratitude, have no one to whom to direct their thanks!

But, it is important that we do some real heart-searching to be sure that our Thanksgiving observance is really sincere.

In the days of Amos (700 B.C.), the prophet, speaking for the Lord, warned Israel about religious hypocrisy, especially in regard to the observance of great national feast days. Israel was accused of coming to the festive service with a heart far away from God. The people loved opportunity to get together, supposedly to thank their God, and there were many sacrifices, many prayers, wonderful music, and the burning of incense, but God was not pleased. They were going through outward annual observances without letting God draw closer for His inner blessing. When the feasts were over they were no closer to Him than they had been before. They had made a holiday out of a holy day.

How sobering are God's words, ". . . this people draw near with their mouth and honor me with their lips, while their hearts are far from me . . ." (Isaiah 29:13). In Christ's day the same rebuke was given, this time by Christ Himself. How about us, of the present day? Can we imagine that Christ is satisfied with our celebrating or does He find it necessary to repeat those same accusing words? How about your own private celebrating and mine?

I am concerned about the greater, lasting spiritual value of our Thanksgiving Day, its afterglow! I believe this could be kindled, if we prayerfully prepared and planned for a spiritual blessing, especially that the table talk at our feast include mention of our heritage. Why not speak of the faith and gratitude of the early settlers, of their thanksgiving even in times of severest trials! Why not speak of the action of our congress in setting aside this day for annual national observance? Why not read the psalmist's call to give thanks? Let us remember that religion is caught as well as taught. God-fearing families can dramatize today, as families have through the centuries, that God is in their midst, ready to accept thanks.

Thoughts to Make Your Day Glow

Always give thanks for everything to our God and Father in the name of our Lord Jesus Christ.

Ephesians 5:20, LIVING LETTERS

Let your lives overflow with joy and thanksgiving for all He has done.

Colossians 2:7, LIVING LETTERS

Don't be weary in prayer; keep at it; watch for God's answers and remember to be thankful when they come.

Colossians 4:2, LIVING LETTERS

Christmas Day

For a number of years, as I have prepared Christmas messages, I have found it stimulating to concentrate on just one person or group of persons connected with the birth of Christ.

58

One year, I traced the lives and activities of shepherds in ancient lands and their significance at the coming of the Saviour to Bethlehem. Another year, I concentrated on angels: all that the Bible teaches about angelic beings and how they ministered to those who were connected with the birth of Christ. Another study I found refreshing and rewarding was that of the doxologies sung at His coming. This year, as I think about the Christ child, a message comes to me about light and darkness.

As we go back 2,000 years, we see a dark world desperately in need of help. Man was hopeless, yearning for freedom, for love; disillusioned yet somehow anticipating some form of help. Ignorance of God and His promises cast more darkness over the situation. The psalmist had said, "Our help is in the name of the Lord, who made heaven and earth," but the masses had ignored these instructions and found themselves wondering when and how help would come. Men were slaves, unloved, sick; life was cheap. Who could do anything about this situation? Would a king come with powerful armies to throw off oppression? Would a heroic, powerful figure come, who could demand loyalty and unite the world? Would a wise, learned scribe come—one who had all the answers to life's puzzling questions? In the days of Isaiah, the Lord chided His people for consulting mediums and wizards and the dead for answers, instead of consulting their God. They looked to the earth, but beheld only the darkness and gloom of anguish and distress (19–22). Then the promise was repeated through Isaiah, to God's faithful ones that One would come, sent of God, to dispel the darkness. As if it were already accomplished, the message went out, "The people who walked in darkness have seen a great light; those who dwelt in a land of deep darkness, on them has light shined" (9:2).

And then, when the time was ripe God sent His promised help—a baby Boy! Certainly, this was not what the world had expected, nor did they accept Him. "How incredible," said men and straightaway despised and rejected God's plan. The world needed help. God sent a Baby—and His plan!

But the story does not end here. This Christ grew up and, when He came to be thirty years of age, He went throughout the land declaring, ". . . I am the light of the world; he who follows me will not walk in darkness, but will have the light of life" (John 8:12). John, also wrote, "And this is the judgment, that the light has come into the world, and men loved darkness rather than light, because their deeds were evil" (3:19). Again Jesus pleaded with His generation, ". . . The light is with you for a little longer. Walk while you have the light, lest the darkness overtake you; he who walks in the darkness does not know where he goes. While you have the light, believe in the light, that you may become sons of light" (12:35–36).

After preaching and teaching for three years, the man, Jesus, tried in one more way to convince men that they were loved of God and that each one of them was precious to Him. Willingly, He went to the cross to die for them. He would rise again on the third day in victory. Finally, he would come again as the Judge of all the earth. The Baby became Teacher, Healer, Saviour, Judge.

Let this be a warning to the once-a-year church attender. For him, Christ is always a Baby. Each year he enjoys again the "Baby Story." It seems to belong to Christmas. What an awakening such a one will have when he must stand one day before Him, who is now King of Kings and Lord of Lords— his rejected Saviour!

It is twenty centuries since Christ first came to this world. Again, the world needs help and needs it desperately. Mankind is estranged from God, empty, frightened, broken. Again only God's few are aware of the Source of help. The rest of mankind goes heedlessly on. They, too, will celebrate! They, too, will speak of the Baby Jesus. They, too, will give gifts and say to each other, "Merry Christmas." But, within their hearts, there is no merry climate. The Light is not shining. It is dark and clammy. There is no radiance, no growth, just a dead existence! The agony of it is that they do not know what life in the Light can be!

This is our challenge—*tell them*. Demonstrate it, live it, invite them. In our conversations, let us speak of the true Source of Christmas joy. In our churches, let them feel the warmth of Christian love. In our homes, let them see evidence of our faith in Christ, the Saviour and the joy that is ours.

It is so easy to be led by the world into *their* kind of Christmas observance—busyness with multitudes of trifles, no time for Him whose birthday we observe.

It may not be difficult in Christian homes to make the reason we give gifts to each other real to children; to teach them it is because God gave us His best gift, the Saviour, His Son. More difficult is the task of teaching children that today is especially the time for each of us to give our best *to Him*, because, after all, it is *His* birthday. And what is that gift each of us can give? Our hearts!

I love the story of one family, gathered around the Christmas tree, ready to begin their celebration. Before any gift giving began, the father read the Christmas story and they sang carols. Then the father reminded them that the first one who should receive a gift should be Christ, because it was His birthday. After that they would give to each other. What Christ wanted was their hearts.

The older children, together with their mother, had prepared individual red hearts earlier. Now, each child was invited to write his name on his heart, to come to the tree and to hang his heart in a choice spot saying, "Lord Jesus, I give You my heart as Your birthday present. I want You to live in my heart." They all sang

> Ah, dearest Jesus, holy child
> Make thee a bed, soft, undefiled

61

Within my heart, that it may be
A quiet chamber kept for thee.

Von Himmel Hoch, MARTIN LUTHER

Now they were ready to receive gifts from each other.

Thoughts to Make Your Day Glow

God saw a crushed bruised world at His doorstep.
  It thought it needed Things.
        He gave them: a Baby to love
                      a Man to follow
                      a Saviour to worship
                      a Life to share.

At Christmas God offers anew His everlasing love to all
mankind; man is free to accept peace—Heaven.

16
TO GOD

Life is lived at its best when we learn to trust. In our kind of world, people and situations are imperfect, we make ourselves and each other unhappy, and worries are inevitable. Although we need to struggle with fear and anxiety daily, we need not be defeated by them.

Do you realize it is possible to be released from worry? It is not only possible, God expects it and commands it. Both in the Hebrew Scriptures and in the New Testament God offered to help us if we would take our problems to Him.

Someone said, "There are 365 'Fear Nots' in the Bible—one for every day in the year. How dare we then fear!"

The time will never come when you will have no worries. Even Jesus said, "In the world you have tribulation," then He added, "but be of good cheer, I have overcome the world" (John 16:33). Note that he uses the word "overcome," not "escape."

"Overcome" does not say that one can do it by himself. Willpower is not the tool, trust is—trust in Him, who is always as near as our need, always willing and able to help. He has overcome the whole problem of sin and suffering. As we remain close to Him we too shall overcome. Alone, yet not alone, we walk through each day. Attacked by fears, remind yourself of the Presence with you. Flee to Him for help and release.

The classic lesson on overcoming worry is found in Philippians 4:6 (KJV): "Be careful for nothing; but in every thing by prayer and supplication with thanksgiving let your requests be made known unto God."

This lesson is preceded by the call to that abundant life of rejoicing in the Lord *always*. We are not asked to rejoice in troubles; God does not expect the impossible of us. But we *are* asked to rejoice *in Him* always—even in times of trouble. Memorize this formula and use it constantly as an antidote to worry. Notice the fourfold content of this antidote.

1. "Be careful for nothing. . . ." That word "nothing" may startle us. We may be able to understand that we are to leave the little daily cares with Him, but surely this big problem that has overpowered us is an exception! Silently, firmly, God's word answers, "Not even this. There are no exceptions." Is anything too hard for the Lord? Will your worry help solve the problem? Won't worry cloud your thinking and shatter your nerves, so you will be less able to cope with it? Before the word "nothing" we can only bow in submission and say, "Lord, you will have to show us how to trust. Increase our faith."

2. ". . . with thanksgiving. . . ." Only thankful children of God see what resources they have at hand. Thanksgiving is a hallowing of God's name, and it serves us in a twofold way. It decreases the size and threat of our present problem, as we compare it with God's greatness and goodness as He has revealed it to us in the past; it dissolves bitterness, self-pity and resentment, all of which are barriers separating us from God.

3. ". . . by prayer and supplication. . . ." This step is so simple: "Ye have not because ye ask not. . . . Ask, and it shall be given you. . . . Let your requests be made known to God." Tell Him all about it. Do not withhold one item from Him. Tell Him your secret desires and motives; do not polish up or excuse your sins. "The Lord is nigh unto all them that call upon him, to all that call upon him in truth" (Psalm 145:18, KJV).

Telling it to another will help bring contrition. Help comes also from getting it off your chest. Look at your trouble at arm's length and it will not crush you. Prayer changes you.

Remember, God does not need to be coaxed. If a thing is right and good for you, He wants you to have it even before you ask for it. On the other hand, if you want something that will harm you, or the one for whom you are interceding, God will in mercy withhold it, no matter how much you coax and plead. He loves you too much to let you add to your problem. Do not approach Him as one seeking to bend an unwilling God to your plea, rather stand silently in His presence, willing to bend your will to His best plan.

4. ". . . let your requests be made known unto God." Pray without ceasing. Let us suppose you awake this morning with a great burden that fills you with fear and misgivings. Afflictions come to all of us; it is no sin to fear danger and to want release. But it *is* sin to hug this worry to your heart for even an hour, when you have the privilege of taking it to God immediately.

If you do go to God with it immediately, and come from the place of prayer released, quiet, trusting, do not be surprised if anxiety recurs before the morning is over. What to do? Pray again. This time, not about your problem—He has heard that and is already answering. Praise Him for that; and pray about yourself. Admit that your fear has returned and ask Him to forgive you and release you again. You may need to do this a number of times, but that is what your heavenly Father approves. Remember the admonition, "Pray without ceasing" (I Thessalonians 5:17, KJV). Then your burden will turn into a blessing, for anything that makes you lean harder and oftener on God is a blessing. Romans 8:28 will become a reality: ". . . in everything God works for good with those who love him . . ." You will thank God for the burden, because it is bringing you nearer to Him. All bitterness will be gone if you abide in Him.

Times will come when release will not come even after repeated prayer—when you do not seem able to pray through to assurance and release. Your Master, in His infinite love, made provision for such times by encouraging prayer-partnership. Find a believing friend, pour out your heart before him, talk over possible solutions, agree upon what you want to ask of God and in joint prayer pray through. "Again I say unto you, that if two of you shall agree on earth as touching any thing that they shall ask, it shall be done for them of my Father which is in heaven" (Matthew 18:19, KJV). Blessed is the man who has such a friend.

Mark's Gospel ends with encouraging words: ". . . the Lord working with them" (KJV). "With them" suggests that you have to do *your* part to fight worry. Your part is to do anything that will take your thoughts away from your trouble after you have committed it to God. Leave it with Him. Deliberately, fill your mind with other thoughts—of work, of friends; read a good book; see a shut-in. Do anything to help erase your fear-thought. Try to recall trust-thoughts from the Bible and give them a chance to come to the surface with their healing power. When peace comes into your heart, you will know that you have overcome. This can be your daily experience in His strength.

Thoughts to Make Your Day Glow

Your Master knows no fear and He expects you to fear nothing while He is with you.

. . . Call upon me in the day of trouble; I will deliver thee, And thou shalt glorify me (Psalm 50:15, KJV).

Cast thy burden upon the Lord, and He shall sustain thee (Psalm 55:22, KJV).

No man ever sank under the burden of the day. It is when tomorrow's burden is added to the burden of today that the weight is more than a man can bear.

GEORGE MACDONALD

17
TO SELF

Why can't we live happy lives, when the world is so beautiful and we are surrounded by God's goodness? Hymn writer, Reginald Heber used strong but true language when he penned the words "Though every prospect pleases, And only man is vile." Man is his own worse enemy. "Self" can be a cruel tyrant.

One evening, a group of women were discussing a mutual friend. Said one, "I don't understand it. She has everything that should make a person happy—health, home, a kind husband and children, more security and skills than most of us have; yet she is always unhappy."

Said a second, "Yes, and she is a Christian too, a praying Christian. I don't get it. What is wrong?"

Then a third spoke, "I think I know, and what I am going to say, I want to say in kindness and without judging, because I love her. I think it is *too much self*." That was the correct diagnosis—too much self!

Those who counsel unhappy people tell us that many causes of unhappiness lie in what people bring to life, rather than what life brings to people. Many well-adjusted persons, who live adventuresome lives, have limitations, trials and handicaps, but they have learned the secret of great living.

Let us look at the Bible's instructions for selfless, Christian living. "Let each of you look not only to his own interests, but also to the interests of others" (Philippians 2:4).

In one of our beloved hymns we find the words, "I look not inward. That would make me wretched." It is possible to have a wrong life-direction by looking too much at self. To be sure, we need to do some heart-searching and problem-facing, but we are not to concentrate abnormally on our own interests and desires—a sure way to become wretched.

Life will lose its freshness and bounce, if we spend our days selfishly guarding our own comforts, our own pleasures, our own chances to get ahead or to become important. We will become a problem to ourselves and to those with whom we live and work if we let self-pity creep in. We will become unreasonable, suspicious, unlovely, scatter gloom and make this world a harder place in which to live.

Even our praying may become selfish if we forget that Jesus did not teach us to pray, "My Father . . . give *me* . . . forgive *me*. . . ." He said, "Father . . . give *us*" In selfish prayer, we rob ourselves of the joy of carrying many others to the throne of grace with us.

The inevitable result of living an ingrown life is a downcast spirit, frustration, weariness, restlessness, tension. We cannot break God's laws of health and not suffer consequences.

It is no use thinking "If only other people and my circumstances would change, then I could be happy." The source of trouble lies in our own wrong life-direction. Freed from the bondage of selfishness, we will receive a cheerful heart and its inevitable healing. "A cheerful heart is a good medicine . . ." (Proverbs 17:22).

If you are a slave to yourself, at some point in your earlier life you yielded to yourself instead of to God. It may be hard for you to change, but the moment you are willing for God to alter your disposition, His re-creating forces will begin to work. He can bring the necessary change when you begin to help answer your own prayers. The only way you can do that is to look to the interests of others. Be concerned about their happiness, not just yours. You will find that bringing happiness to others is like perfume; you can't give to others without getting a breath of it yourself. You will be surprised how happy your days will become. Try it. You have nothing to lose but ugliness, and everything to gain—God's approval, your neighbor's love and your own increased capacity to live.

Now go and tell some young person about your discovery and start him on the way that leads to selfless living.

But it is not enough to look away from self to others. We need to look to the Source of newness of life—Christ. Without Him we are anemic. In physical anemia, blood transfusions are used to help restore the body health. In spiritual anemia, God uses the same method in an unseen mysterious way. The blood of Christ enters into our penitent hearts and the condition of anemia becomes changed into one of vibrant, tireless vitality. Christ unites Himself with you in a life union as close as that of the vine and the branch. He comes to live in you and to lead you from strength to strength.

In His Presence we get a truer sense of values. What seemed all-important before, now takes its rightful size and place, and we wonder how we could have cared so much about trifles. Where we were nervous and sickly, we now radiate well-being.

71

An irresistable power emanates from a well-directed life. A radiant person, without realizing it, is saying, "I commend Christ and Christian living to you. It is wonderful."

Thoughts to Make Your Day Glow

People who are wrapped up in themselves make small packages.

Refuse to be held at the level of the commonplace. Soar to heights.

He that scatters thorns, let him go barefoot.

18
TO OTHERS

Be a Barnabas

"Everyone needs a Barnabas" was our pastor's topic for a confirmation service. In order to gain the significance of this message we need to ask, "What or who is a Barnabas?" Obviously, it is the name of a person. We meet him several times in the story of the early church. We are introduced to him in connection with Saul, who through a personal encounter with Christ at the walls of Damascus became a changed man. When Paul returned to Jerusalem as a new convert, the apostles at the church there were afraid of him; they remembered him as one of those who had stoned Stephen. They could not believe that he was now one of the New Way. Only one person had faith in him—Barnabas. He took Paul before the apostles and assured them of his turnabout. The name Barnabas means "son of encouragement." And well he played his role!

But Paul was not given a warm reception in Jerusalem and he left for his home in Tarsus. Later, who was it who went searching for Paul? Again, it was our friend Barnabas.

In Acts 15, Paul invited Barnabas to accompany him on his second missionary journey. Barnabas agreed, provided that John Mark go along as a third companion. Paul refused. And Barnabas again was the understanding one. He saw a great potential in John Mark and realized that John Mark needed encouragement. So Barnabas took John Mark and went on his way, while Paul took Silas.

What if Barnabas had not encouraged John Mark? We might never have had the second gospel, which is so full of trustful information about our Lord Jesus Christ! Thus the lives of both Paul and John Mark were made significant because of the encouragement of Barnabas.

We all need a Barnabas, someone who believes in us and encourages us. This is what Christian friends are to be to each other.

Not only are Christian friends to encourage each other, they are also to encourage him who has no friends, who is defeated, who feels worthless, rejected, who would welcome a chance to prove his worth.

Are you willing to be a Barnabas to such a one? Have you ever thanked God for the Barnabases who have crossed your path—who gave you self-respect, confidence and who knowing all about you, still loved you?

But there is another Barnabas—the church—which has been an encourager to you and to me. The church has urged us on to make the most of our lives for Christ's sake; the church, as the fellowship of believers, has been a source of strength to us.

The church is not a program; it is God's redeemed people to whom the one and only commandment was given—to scatter love. This church still lives by the gospel and therefore she is the custodian of the Word of God.

There are those who say the church of today has nothing to give, that it has failed its mission, that the content of the Bible is questionable and that perhaps even God Himself needs changing!

For all who think thus, the church has one magnificent answer, Christ's own words, "Heaven and earth shall pass away, but my words shall not pass away" (Matthew 24:35, KJV).

That's final! In this truth the church trusts.

Thoughts to Make Your Day Glow

Fear not little flock, for it is your Father's good pleasure to give you the kingdom (Luke 12:32).

Strong beliefs win strong men, and then make them stronger.

WALTER BAGEHOT

Be an Intercessor

I have just completed reading two books which depict the working of the underground church in countries behind the iron curtain. As I read of the suffering and anguish of our fellow-believers in these lands, I was ashamed that I had been so uninformed and, therefore, so indifferent to their plight. Over and over again I said to myself, "If I, like those Christians, were languishing in a dark, lonely prison cell, how I would wish that fellow-believers around the world would know and care what is happening to me."

In my ears rang the words, "Bear ye one another's burdens . . ." (Galatians 6:2, KJV). ". . . as ye have done it unto one of the least of these my brethren, ye have done it unto me . . . I was . . . in prison and ye visited me not" (Matthew 25:40, 43, KJV).

My total inability to go to them in person, and my total inability to effect any relief, overwhelmed me until these words came tumbling into my consciousness: ". . . The prayer of a righteous man has great power in its effects" (James 5:16). "If ye shall ask anything . . . I will do it" (John 14:14, KJV). ". . . Peter was kept in prison; but earnest prayer for him was made to God by the church" (Acts 12:5).

Here was my assignment—earnest prayer! I cannot go to the oppressed people but my prayers can! I cannot unlock prison doors, but God will use my prayers to unlock them. My prayers can penetrate the highest wall, the darkest dungeon. Necessity is laid upon me to pray.

But how does God use my prayers? He knows where each of the millions of today's martyrs are confined; He knows each one by name; He knows how much torture each one can bear before the breaking point. In answer to my prayer He will come with His aid. Some will be set free. Others will have to go through ordeals, but He will be at their sides; they will feel His Presence and have joy in their hearts in spite of pain and deprivation.

It is unbelievable what man can do to man, what devilish methods he can use to torture. One can hardly bear to read about it, much less imagine what it must feel like. All I can say is, "Lord, have mercy upon them. Somehow help them to know that we care and that You are there."

It is thrilling to read of the heroic effort of the underground church to bring Bibles to congregations, deprived of their last copy. These Christians risk their lives to deliver each copy. We are told that when a Bible does get through, it is cut into sections and distributed among the flock so each can copy a gospel or epistle for his own use. On Sundays the sections are returned to the pastor and redistributed.

I heard an American church leader tell how he received an envelope from a faithful pastor behind the iron curtain. Letters were censored. What dared he write? In the most eloquent language of all he told of their oneness in Christ; he enclosed one communion wafer—nothing more—but the wafer was broken. The enemies of Christ had done their worst, but that broken wafer told the whole story. "We are suffering. Pray for us."

It touched me to tears!

We can enter into this desperate situation through intercession; we may know for certain that someone is stronger, someone comforted, someone freed because we have prayed and

76

God has acted. Each day counts for double, as we seek to live not only for ourselves but for them.

Do not hesitate to take on the burden of others. It gives wings to life!

Thoughts to Make Your Day Glow

If any life of mine may ease
The burden of another,
God give me love and care and strength
To help my ailing brother.

A brother's suff'rings claim a brother's pity.

JOSEPH ADDISON

19
TO MY COUNTRY

Where did the thought originate that patriotism is old-fashioned and unworthy of modern man? Certainly not in the minds of those citizens who are diligently working to make their home and community a better place in which to live. Doesn't it come from those who are not making their contribution to creative living and who are leaning on the Establishment to support them? As long as man thinks of his country as "they" and not "we," there is no hope of community solidarity.

To be sure, we Christians are citizens of two countries—the Kingdom of God and the nation in which we live. We pledge allegiance to both. As citizens of the Kingdom we "pledge allegiance to the Christian flag and to the Saviour for whose Kingdom it stands, one Saviour, crucified, risen and coming again with life and liberty for all who believe." At the same time we "pledge allegiance to the flag of the United States of America and to the republic for which it stands, one nation, under God, indivisible, with liberty and justice for all."

What is there to love about our country? In our national anthem, we freely admit that God needs to mend our flaws. Yes, our nation has its flaws, many and serious, but that is because every one of its leaders and every one of its citizens has flaws. We, like all other nations, are a nation of imperfect people and we live in imperfect harmony.

In spite of imperfection, there is much to love in our land. I love its fertile plains, its mountains and lakes, its trees and flowers, its people. It is interesting to observe how citizens from a treeless area love it because the horizon is so broad and the sunsets so visible; people from the Middle West love their tall corn and their ten thousand lakes; people from the South their cactus or cotton fields; people from mountain areas, the grandeur and majesty within their view. You love what is a delight to you where you are, I where I am. Put it all together and we have a wonderful composite—our *country*!

I love its heritage, its history, its settlers, who loved liberty, who looked to God for guidance, who established a nation under God with the ideal of liberty and justice for all—a nation developed by frontiersmen and women of courage and diligence, built into a great nation among nations, a leader in many noble enterprises, a republic!

I am thankful for all it offers me: my freedom, my protection, a chance to follow my calling; for schools and colleges, churches and libraries. I am thankful for its music, art, literature; its concern about my health, my standard of living, my latter years.

A woman who worked in a foreign country for a number of years and returned home to her native land, related how stunned she was to see the drastic changes—the violence, delinquency, and disrespect. For months, she struggled with disappointment, shame, and diminished love of her country. She became a house divided against itself, because she couldn't live here and not love this land.

Finally, she was able to understand that all America was not like that. She realized that most of our citizens do not approve of those who are disrupting our highest ideal and that each person needs to begin with himself to do a better job of citizenship. In spite of the many disturbing elements, there is much that can be redeemed with the help of God.

Today, that woman loves her country again, and she is happy to be permitted to make her contribution to mend its flaws.

Could it be that on our national holidays we need fewer speeches and more time on our knees? Less bragging and more repentance?

Thoughts to Make Your Day Glow

Blessed is the nation whose God is the Lord . . . (Psalm 33:12).

It is impossible to govern the world without God.

GEORGE WASHINGTON

Whatever makes men good Christians makes them good citizens.

DANIEL WEBSTER

I say the real and permanent grandeur of these States must be their religion.

WALT WHITMAN

20
TO OUTER SPACE

What a thrilling age we are privileged to live in. We cannot comprehend it when we are told that the sun is 93 million miles away, and the next nearest star 26 million million miles away, or that a cluster of stars are 30,000 light years away and that it takes 320 years for the light to cross from one side of the group to the other. Yet these very words fill us with humble reverence. After every new discovery in space we can only join with the hymn writer in saying, "how great Thou art."

It was in 1885 that Carl Boberg, a young Swedish pastor, trekking through a thunderstorm after a church meeting, was inspired to write the words later translated into English:

> O Lord my God! When I in awesome wonder
> Consider all the works thy hands have made,
> I see the stars, I hear the mighty thunder,
> Thy power throughout the universe displayed.

What would Boberg add if he were here today, watching men walk on the moon and come back, and listening to them tell of wondrous sights!

Many people ask, "Is it worth all the money being spent in our generation?" I can't answer that question, but I am sure that with all the new information gained, God is glorified!

At a time when newspapers and magazines were full of space information, I overheard a delightful conversation. Said a young woman, "I simply can't understand where space ends. First we look with our naked eyes and the heavenly bodies seem terribly far away. Then scientists look through telescopes and find that there is still more space. Now they tell us that the giant 200-inch one on Mount Palomar, California, can see into space over a billion light years. There seems to be space upon space and still more space. Where does space end?"

All were silent. Then an older woman said with a hushed voice, "I suppose space will finally end in the very presence of God Himself." That seemed to satisfy the questioner.

I wonder if we are giving today's young people enough of a vision of what is great. Are we exciting their curiosity to search out things which are lasting and sublime? Are we developing their taste for great music, great paintings, great literature? Are we introducing them to the stars, the planets, the constellations? Or are our conversations trivial, dealing only with what is meaningless and passing?

Whenever I have a chance. I encourage parents to give a boy or girl a good book on stars, with the hope that some interest will be aroused for further exploration on the subject. Let's fill the void of their leisure hours with something broadening!

In his book *God's Stars*, my friend Fritz A. Callies combines scientific facts and Biblical information about stars in a refreshing way. He begins his book by asking his readers the question, "Would you like to have a few of God's stars as your very own friends?" What a thought, to have God's stars as friends! He goes on to say, "In Hebrews 2:8 we learn that God wants us to have them." Imagine the fun a family could have, sitting around a table together, drawing lines from dot to dot in a map of the sky (like a follow-the-dot-picture puzzle), creating one of the eighty-eight constellations of stars. Then they could go outdoors, sky map in hand, to identify the stars in the night sky! If you worry about family solidarity, try a project like this one!

Too many of us are satisfied if we can locate the big dipper and the little dipper. How fulfilling it is to add even one new friend in the sky.

When the first men approached the moon overcome with the grandeur of it all, one astronaut read the immortal words, "In the beginning God created the heavens and earth." He could have gone on and quoted, "He made the stars also."

The heavens are telling the glory of God; and the firmament proclaims his handiwork (Psalm 19:1).

O Lord, our Lord, how majestic is thy name in all the earth! . . . When I look at thy heavens, the work of thy fingers, the moon and the stars which thou hast established; what is man that thou art mindful of him, and the son of man that thou dost care for him (Psalm 8:1, 3–4).

O give thanks to the Lord, for he is good, for his steadfast love endures forever. . . . to him who by understanding made the heavens. . . . to him who made the great lights . . . the sun to rule over the day . . . the moon and stars to rule over the night . . . (Psalm 136:1,5,7,8,9).

He determines the number of the stars, he gives to all of them their names (Psalm 147:4).

[God] who made the Bear and Orion, the Pleiades and the chambers of the south. . . . Can you find out the deep things of God? Can you find out the limit of the Almighty? It is higher than heaven. . . . longer than the earth, and broader than the sea (Job 9:9, 11:7–8,9).

Where were you when I laid the foundation of the earth? Tell me, if you have understanding. . . . Can you bind the chains of the Pleiades, or loose the cords of Orion? Can you lead forth the Mazzaroth [signs of Zodiac] or can you guide the Bear with its children (Job 38:4,31–32)?

Having read so much about the Gemini flight, it is fascinating to read in Acts 28, Paul's account of his journey; how he and his companions set sail in an Alexandrian ship, which had a figurehead of the twins Pollux and Castor—the Gemini.

The author of *God's Stars* told me that Roman soldiers used the expression "by Gemini" to make a vow.

The last book of the Bible gives us this instruction, ". . . worship him who made heaven and earth, the sea and the fountains of water" (Revelation 14:7). And now, having finished this earthly life, having worshiped the God of all creation, what will we behold when we finally stand in His Presence by His Grace, to behold not only Him but endless space?

Thoughts to Make Your Day Glow

The stars rule men but God rules the stars.

CHRISTOPH CELLARIUS

Two things fill the mind with ever new and increasing wonder and awe—the starry heavens above me and the moral law within me.

IMMANUEL KANT

Ye stars, that are the poetry of heaven!

GEORGE GORDON, LORD BYRON

Then stars arise, and the night is holy.

HENRY WADSWORTH LONGFELLOW

21
TO INNER SPACE

A little girl was deeply troubled. At the supper table her parents had discussed in detail the subject of transplants. They had spoken of the giving and receiving of human eyes, hearts and lungs. Now at her bedside, she had prayed, "Come into my heart, Lord Jesus, there is room in my heart for Thee." As her mother turned off the light and proceeded to the door, the child called, "Mother I have to ask you something." Wisely, the mother did not ignore this call for help; she sat down on the edge of the bed to listen to the little thinker.

"Mother, I have been wondering and wondering. Where in me is me? In what part of my body is me?" her daughter asked.

How was the mother to answer this profound question? With a quick prayer, "Lord, help me to say the right thing," she repeated the question slowly. "Where in me is me?" Then, hesitantly, she began, "Well, Darling, if it were possible to look inside of you the real you could not be seen. It is not visible. It is like your thoughts. Can you see thoughts?"

A shake of the head and a brightening of the eyes encouraged the mother to go on. "The real you is also in your feelings but you can't see them, can you? Did you see the hurt you felt when you broke your leg or when you cut your hand?"

The little girl said, "No, but I was there because I felt it."

"Were you in your leg, were you in your hand?"

"Yes," the child replied positively. Then a light dawned, "I suppose me is in all of me."

"That's right. You live in this body—your body—in all of it," the mother said, and the child dropped off to sleep satisfied.

The subject of *inner* space is before us. Newspapers and

85

magazines tell us that after we have explored outer space more and more, we must explore the vast unknown areas of inner space. Mankind has neglected to grow in its capacity to improve inner space, to heal its ills and to produce better people. The result is unhappy living, unhappy families, communities full of crime and corruption, death and destruction, nations at war with each other. The big questions are: *What has gone wrong in man's inner being? What can be done to improve man and his relations with others?*

Before we seek to answer these questions, we must remind ourselves that the subject of inner space is not a new one. We have the eternal Word of Him who made the universe and created man. Centuries ago, He told us about inner space, inner health, inner beauty and inner peace. He told us how to care for our inner life as well as for our outer well-being. He had to give us help in both areas because we are total beings. We cannot have sick emotions and a well body; neither can we think wrong thoughts without physical tensions. *Thoughts Have Consequences* was the title of a book I read some time ago. How true this statement is! We could add that desires, memories and ambitions also have consequences.

What has gone wrong? Too many people have not availed themselves of the information in our Scriptures, on the subject of inner well-being. In ignorance, they have thought up substitutes for finding happiness. They are not aware that in every human heart God has reserved a vacancy only He can fill. James wrote to the early Christians:

What is causing the quarrels and fights among you? Isn't it because there is a whole army of evil desires within you?

You want what you don't have so you kill to get it. You long for what others have, and can't afford it, so you start a fight to take it away from them. And yet the reason you don't have what you want is because you don't ask God for it.

86

And when you do ask you don't get it because your whole aim is wrong—you want only what will give *you* pleasure (4:1–3, LIVING LETTERS).

The Bible uses the word "heart" to express our inner space, our inner self. The heart is looked upon as the source of understanding, the seat of our emotions, of our desires, of good and evil. Jesus once said, "For out of the heart come evil thoughts, murder, adultery, fornication, theft, false witness, slander" (Matthew 15:19).

There are many ways of speaking about our inner condition: "a good and honest heart," "a broken heart," "a clean heart," "an evil heart," "a hardened heart."

The heart is the seat of man's *believing*. "For it is by believing in his heart that a man becomes right with God . . ." (Romans 10:10, LIVING LETTERS). ". . . I pray that Christ will be more and more at home in your hearts, living within you as you trust in Him" (Ephesians 3:17, LIVING LETTERS).

The heart is the seat of our *thoughts*. The psalmist prayed, "Search me, O God, and know my heart! Try me and know my thoughts!" (Psalm 139:23).

The heart is also the seat of our *imaginations*. "He has shown strength with his arm, he has scattered the proud in the imagination of their hearts" (Luke 1:51).

The heart is also the abode of *peace*. "And let the peace of Christ rule in your hearts . . . (Colossians 3:15).

What can be done? Let us use the information we have on hand. The Bible tells us that if our hearts are soiled, they need cleansing, and for that forgiveness is available. This is the Good News. Neglected guilt leads to serious consequences. The healing balm is the assurance, the deep certainty of God's pardon, of our chance to make a new start. If our hearts are filled with envy, hostility, greed, the Bible tells us we will have unhappy lives. But it also tells us that we cannot change ourselves; we need to confess our inability to handle

87

our feelings and to accept release through the Power of Christ's Spirit working in us.

When will nations learn that same truth? The writer of Proverbs gives us this insight, "When the righteous are in authority, the people rejoice; but when the wicked rule, the people groan" (29:2). Who are the righteous? They who are right with God, right with their fellow men and right with themselves. These are the people we should put into office, that they might be led of God. When both leaders and people neglect to seek God's will and to do it, we find exactly what the writer of the Proverb said, "the people groan." We are groaning today, and many are blaming God for our trouble.

A highly educated and sophisticated woman sat at a dinner table near me. During an animated conversation, she said, "My faith in God is getting weaker and weaker. I used to think God ruled the world, but when I see all the evils in it, the war and all the bloodshed, I begin to lose interest in Him." This woman was groaning—accusing God for man's neglect.

She seemed relieved when I said, "Don't blame God. He told us to love one another and to bear one another's burdens. He is grieved that we, His children, disobey His instructions so flagrantly. His one and great commandment was to love as He loved. We have hated as He forbade."

"Yes, I guess you are right," she admitted. "I guess it is our fault and not His."

Our minds belong to God. Let us open them up to Him and let Him fill them with His fullness.

Then let men explore the *how* of living out God's instructions!

Thoughts to Make Your Day Glow

The heart of a good man is the sanctuary of God in this world.

MADAME NECKER

None but God can satisfy the longings of an immortal soul; that as the heart was made for Him, so He only can fill it.

RICHARD CHENEVIX TRENCH

God has two dwellings: one in heaven, and the other in a meek and thankful heart.

IZAAK WALTON

. . . Heart, be thou the sunflower, not only open to receive God's blessing, but constant in looking to him.

JEAN PAUL RICHTER

IV
Every Undertaking
of Life

22
MINISTRY OF RECONCILIATION

Is there a day in our lives in which we do not undertake something? To meet the needs of the family, to fulfill daily assignments at the office, to be active in community service or church activities? Each of these undertakings, if we are aware of its value in the total process of individual and group living, can remove boredom and add a glow of fulfillment. Clean clothes neatly folded dramatizes successful effort for the family. Anticipating the result of any effort gives bounce to otherwise routine days.

If this is true in everyday undertakings, it is true also in the great undertakings involving mankind. Let us think, for example, of the ministry of reconciliation. Two thousand years ago, our Lord said, "Happy are those who work for peace among men; God will call them his sons!" (Matthew 5:9, TEV).

As you well know, peacemaking among men is not a great noble undertaking that is accomplished once, for a lifetime. It is a daily ministry, never completed. Each day presents possibilities for new strife or for old ones rekindled.

Count that day heroic, in which you obeyed the commandment of the Lord—through strength from above—and bit off the cutting word that was about to escape your lips.

Count that day a good one, in which you were privileged to turn off angry words others were about to use in hostility.

Count that day well-spent, in which you took time to pray for those in positions of world leadership who are seeking to bring peace to a war-weary world.

Count that day priceless, in which you were able to help a racist see the dignity of every human life regardless of color; count it more so if you yourself gained a victory in this area.

In deep contrition and humility let me tell you of a seemingly insignificant experience, which blew some fresh air into my stuffy, strangling judgmental attitude. Until this day, whenever I saw a dirty, unkempt, long-haired individual, I had the urge to communicate disgust—clearly!

On this particular day, a long-haired, bearded man, in filthy clothes, was way ahead of me in a long line at the checkout counter of a supermarket. I wanted to say, "Man alive, why don't you clean up like the rest of us nice people?" But, twenty minutes earlier, I had left the United States Congress of Evangelism where we had heard, again and again, how much *all* men need Christ's love and our understanding; how we were to begin with those whose lives evidently lacked fulfillment. Shame filled my heart, when I realized that at that very moment I was carrying a condemning attitude, a better-than-thou feeling. I prayed, "Oh, Lord have patience with me and give me patience with this man. Here is one of those about whom we have been speaking and praying. This very moment, change my attitude."

Then a wonderful thing happened. As soon as I offered God my willingness to love, He supplied the power. I stopped thinking of soap and water; I just wanted to look into this man's face and to smile at him. Another shopper, wishing to cut across the line of customers, pushed me within touching nearness of him. I looked into his eyes, which were mild and kind, and said as kindly as I could, "Pardon me, I guess someone pushed me." Not a very profound thing to say, but I wanted to say something to him.

He looked me in the eye, smiled a warm, winning smile and, stretching forth his hand, offered me the trading stamps he had just received from the cashier. "May I give these to you?" he asked. "Perhaps you save them."

I wanted to prolong the conversation, in order to have a chance to witness to him, so I said, "Thank you. But don't you have opportunity to use them?"

He smiled again and replied, "Oh, I am only passing through and have no use for them." Then he joined the crowd hurrying out of the store and I watched him run down the street, a package of oatmeal in one hand.

It all happened so fast I was unable to do more. I was comforted however by the thought that perhaps all he needed, just at that moment, was evidence of acceptance and understanding and goodwill—proof that he was considered worthy of a second thought. Perhaps God will use someone else in our city, or in another city, to communicate acceptance. And perhaps that young man will be just a wee bit more receptive to the gospel because I did not reject him.

As the result of this contact, I want to learn all I can about the message these people are trying to get across to us by their appearance and activities. Someone put their plea into these words, "I want something that cares for me. I want to see change, action." We find this inner loneliness and estrangement from the God who really cares in contemporary songs: "I've got to be me" or "I can't get no satisfaction." Only in Christ can their incompleteness, loneliness, and frightening sense of unfulfillment be met, but God uses men and women like you and me to make His love known. Many have said, "You love humanity but hate people." Do we have a passion for Christ but no compassion for people? Christ does not want us to work *for* him, just to make ourselves available *to* Him so that He can send us out on a mission of reconciliation.

But we must be peacemakers among those of our "in-groups," as well as among those who are strange to us. How many former friends, acquaintances, neighbors, relatives are no

95

longer compatible? How many are avoiding each other or speaking unkindly of each other? When this happens among those who are Christians, it is doubly sad, because it is such a poor witness of Christ's power and love. They may say, "I don't want to see this person again. I am better off avoiding contact because I am too involved emotionally—perhaps later, when the hurt is not so deep." Because we care, we dare not let this situation go on without trying to minister reconciliation. If there is no way to mediate openly, there is always secret prayer; we may ask God to break the power of wrong thinking and to supply the spirit of forgiveness.

Be glad if you have been given the opportunity to be a mediator. It is not your own wisdom that is convincing, but the words of the Master. He gave clear directions on how to climb out of the fog of hostility, into the sunshine of restored love. "But I tell you who hear me: Love your enemies, do good to those who hate you, bless those who curse you, and pray for those who mistreat you" (Luke 6:27-28, TEV).

Take a second look at this counsel of our Lord. First, He tells us to love our enemies. This word "love" does not mean to like. It signifies a compassionate understanding and caring about the welfare and happiness of others. This kind of love is not within us by nature. It is a gift from God and must be asked for. With this kind of love we can have goodwill toward the unlovable ones, and proceed to the next step in the process of restoring peace, namely to do good to those from whom we are estranged. This is a tall order, but the Lord will help us obey as soon as we begin to make the effort honestly. What kind of good is meant? Anything—a kind glance, a smile, a kind word, a phone call, a letter, a visit, some garden flowers, some tasty dish—will say, "I'm thinking kindly of you and want peace between us. This little gift comes to prove it." To keep praying that the hurt will pass away is not enough. The offended one must take a definite step of reconciliation and, as he does so, he will be changed. He will be able to think

kindly again even if his first effort at reconciliation is re-
buffed. In Christ's Presence, he will not be able to say, "I am
so good, he is so bad." A child of God will not be able to let
such words pass his lips. He will want to say, "Help us both."
Now the word "blessed" or "happy" becomes a reality. What a
relief to be right with God and right with everyone else. The
day in which you experience this victory, or help another to it,
will certainly be a day aglow!

Thoughts to Make Your Day Glow

Lord, make me an instrument of Thy peace.
Where there is hatred, let me sow love;
When there is injury, pardon;
Where there is doubt, faith;
When there is despair, hope;
Where there is darkness, light;
When there is sadness, joy.

O Divine Master, grant that
I may not so much seek
To be consoled, as to console;
Not so much to be understood as
To understand; not so much to be
Loved as to love:
For it is in giving that we receive;
It is in pardoning that we are pardoned;
It is in dying that we awaken to eternal life.

FRANCIS OF ASSISI

He who forgives ends the quarrel.

AFRICAN PROVERB

Nothing in this lost and ruined world bears the meek impress of the Son of God so surely as forgiveness.

ALICE CARY

Humanity is never so beautiful as when praying for forgiveness, or else forgiving another.

JEAN PAUL RICHTER

23
MINISTRY OF IDENTIFICATION

An undertaking which never knows completion, is ongoing daily ministry—the ministry of identification. To identify means to treat as the same, or to associate closely, as with a person or group or movement.

Our Lord identified Himself with our human race; He became one of us when He took on human form and He became

98

man so He could sympathize with our weaknesses. He was tempted in every way that we are, but He did not sin. Peter in his letter to early Christians wrote, ". . . Christ himself suffered for you and left you an example, so that you would follow in his steps. . . . When he suffered he did not threaten, but placed his hopes in God, the righteous Judge" (I Peter 2:21,23, TEV).

As Christ identified Himself with man in order to be able to feel as man feels in his life situations, we are to identify ourselves with men of our age in their needs. We are to seek to feel with them, to experience vicariously what they experience, and to offer understanding, acceptance and help.

In Ezekiel we find a perfect example of identification. When he listened to the exiles dwelling by the river, he entered into their feeling of hopelessness: ". . . And I sat there overwhelmed, among them seven days" (3:15). He sat where they sat!

How difficult it is for us to feel as other people feel. In our affluence, we have no way of knowing how it feels not to have money for next month's rent and to have to worry about being evicted. We do not know how it feels to live in a tumble-down shack, where the plumbing does not work and plaster is falling from the ceilings; where wind and rain enter through large cracks; where a child screams in the night because a rat has bitten it. We don't like to read about any of these things, much less see them—they bother us too much. We would not be able to sleep for the horror of it. Of course we care, but only from a distance as spectators. Perhaps we even say, "Why don't they fix their place up as we do?" We forget that their landlord may be a corporation without a heart, or a real estate owner deaf to any plea for improvement. Where would they get their money to pay for it themselves?

When, through God's help, we become able to identify with those who are oppressed and cheated of the simple dignities of human living His Grace opens our eyes to the disgrace of human greed and indifference. Now we care; we agonize; we seek to understand, to communicate our concern, to actually bring help. Like Ezekiel, we sit where they sit and are at last driven to action.

Person-to-person identification is within our reach. Usually, our contacts, our means, our personal action and encouragement can help an unemployed neighbor to continue his fruitful search for work, not to give up. But, when it comes to thousands of hungry, unemployed, sick, impotent brethren, the whole idea seems hopeless. *Now* identification means keeping informed, pressing for legislation and social action. But even this is not enough. Our battlefield lies in the secret of prayer with God's promises before us. It is Satan who holds men in the bondage of selfishness, lust for power, unconcern for others. It is Satan who seeks to hinder all efforts at decency. "For we are not fighting against human beings, but against the wicked spiritual forces . . ." (Ephesians 6:12, TEV). When I pray, in the Lord's prayer, "Deliver us from evil," I am asking God to resist the evil one and every evil system that brings harm to men. Thus I identify before the throne with all who need to be set free from evil.

Individual personal involvement and group involvement is needed to meet the needs of tribes and peoples living in the darkness of paganism. To identify with those who have never heard of Christ, means to try to feel as they feel without knowing about a loving, merciful Saviour; with those who are afraid to live, and afraid to die; with those who are held in horrible tribal superstitions and torturous tribal customs. When they are sick they have no physician for the body; when they are full of guilt, they have no physician for the soul. Never again should we let anyone go unchallenged who says, "Let them alone. They are happy in their own way of living. If they don't want to wear clothes, let them go naked. What's the difference?" Once we have learned from missionaries how these people feel and suffer without hope, it isn't the kind of clothes or lack of them that concerns us, it is the crying need for hope and love and comfort of the gospel. These constrain us to do all we can to bring them the Good News as quickly as possible. Only when we know that they are receiving the gospel and Christian kindness, can we feel the joy that can be theirs. In this feeling of joy, we identify with them also.

Often, we fail in one other area of identification—the area of feeling with our children. They may come running to us, heartbroken because of the loss of a beloved object. In our estimation, the item is utterly valueless, but it is a love-object to them. Too often we dismiss the problem easily because it seems so small to us. But, when we identify, we listen carefully and attentively, trying to feel as the child must feel so that we may offer the understanding and comfort worthy of the occasion, and the help they need at that moment. To say, "Get away, can't you see I'm busy. Don't be a crybaby!" is cruel. The least a parent can do is to listen, and to listen without giving the impression that the child is taking precious time away from vastly more important things. To identify means to let the child feel that there is nothing more important than his hurt at that moment. Perhaps listening is the best and quickest way to enter upon the ministry of identification.

The world is full of people who need to talk out their inner and outer needs. If only someone would listen! In her book, *The Listener*, Taylor Caldwell shows how people can find understanding of their own situations and possible solutions by speaking to someone behind a curtain—someone who listens even though the teller can see no one. Good listening to the experiences of our dear ones builds family solidarity and identification with one another. After a day, or a mealtime of sharing and listening, home seems a hallowed place.

Religion is man's relation to man as the result of man's relation to God.

Anyone can criticize;
Many can organize;
But we need those who will agonize
over those who need Christ.

Many people in ordinary circumstances are millionaires of cheerfulness.
They make their neighborhood brighter, happier, and a better place to live in by their presence;
They raise the value of every lot for blocks around them!

24
MINISTRY OF RENEWAL

"Is our nation on the threshold of judgment or renewal?" This anxiety-question is asked often in my classes. A nation so blessed of God and so estranged from Him, as we are now, could easily expect the judgment of God to fall upon us.

The description of Israel's moral and spiritual condition before the coming of the Saviour fits conditions in our land. In the first chapter of Isaiah, the prophet speaks of a sinful nation, a people laden with iniquity who deal corruptly, who have forsaken the Lord, utterly estranged from the Holy One of Israel. Our nation deals corruptly, too. An inner decay has set in, which threatens everything sacred to us.

But, thank God, all is not lost! As we traverse the length and breadth of our beloved land we find an ever-faithful remnant who is preventing total disintegration—the salt of the earth. These are God's people. These are they who are looking to him with the assurance "our help is in the name of the Lord who made heaven and earth." These are they who dare to resist the evil one and his evil works. These are they who seek wisdom from above to recognize true values. These are they who use the Word of God as a sword, knowing that the Holy Spirit can take any verse and drive it into human hearts; He can shatter complacency and expose man's limited security so that man, in all his bankruptcy, will come to Christ. These are they who abide in Christ, knowing full well that only those who stay close to Christ can help those who are far away from Him. These are they who have a message; therefore God gives them a ministry. It is through this remnant that God may grant us another time of grace. It is encouraging that so many of our national leaders and top scientists fearlessly witness of their faith in Christ. How encouraging it is that effective groups of young people on our campuses tell the Good News fearlessly. Men and women in all walks of life study the Word faithfully, in small and large groups. How encouraging it is to see multitudes flocking to vast crusades, so many yielding their lives to Christ. How encouraging is the hunger for Christian literature. Add to all of these people, the unnumbered crowds of folks longing for someone they do not yet know, eager for something to fill their vacuum. They are ready for the gospel, if only we would hurry to present it

103

to them. If only we knew how to catch their ear and knew how to communicate with them!

There are a number of familiar words used to tell of great help that God sent in the past: revival, renaissance, reformation, awakening, renewal. Peter, in his great temple sermon spoke of "times of refreshing" or "times of spiritual strength." Isn't this what we are all longing for? Like a parched, thirsty land, we yearn for a shower of new strength, beauty and goodness.

In history, progress has always come in waves. The church, too, has moved in waves of spiritual quickening. In the Old Testament often we find Israel on a plateau, maintaining only a lukewarm awareness of God. Then, through the influence of a faithful prophet, or the result of a national calamity, or when the people found and read again the words of their Scriptures, waves of spiritual strength returned.

Our great concern is *when* do such seasons of refreshing come? Can we hasten them on? I suppose the overall answer is that they come when God knows that we are ripe for them. They come from His Presence. Man cannot produce them. No amount of committee meetings, of surveys, of planning sessions can usher in a revival. It is the Holy Spirit who produces renewal. He is like the wind, which blows wherever it wishes; you hear the sound it makes but you do not know where it comes from and where it is going. As the Holy Spirit gets the chance to change individuals, He can use them to influence others. Thus, revival begins with repentance and a turning to God to wipe away sin and its enslavement. Then, and only then, can revival come.

Someone explained it in this way. Before revival can come, man must become tired of *things*; he must experience a great hunger for God, a coming back to the Word of God; he must offer much earnest prayer, and have an expectation that revival is on the way.

Sin must be confessed and turned away from. "Therefore confess your sins to one another, and pray for one another, that you may be healed. The prayer of a righteous man has great power in its effects" (James 5:16). We need to confess the sins of our nation as well as our own sins. In Daniel 9 we learn how to pray for our land.

I prayed to the Lord my God and made confession, saying, "O Lord, the great and terrible God, who keepest covenant and steadfast love with those who love him and keep his commandments, we have sinned and done wrong and acted wickedly and rebelled, turning aside from thy commandments and ordinances. . . . To thee, O Lord, belongs righteousness, but to us confusion of face. . . . To the Lord our God belong mercy and forgiveness. . . . the Lord our God is righteous in all the works which he has done, and we have not obeyed his voice. . . . O Lord, according to all thy righteous acts, let thy anger and thy wrath turn away. . . . hearken to the prayer of thy servant and to his supplications, and for thy own sake, O Lord, cause thy face to shine upon thy sanctuary, which is desolate. O my God, incline thy ear and hear; open thy eyes and behold our desolations. . . . O Lord, hear; O Lord, forgive; O Lord, give heed and act; delay not for thy own sake. . . ."

What a sincere prayer of humble repentance!

The challenge comes to the people of our land, too. Every committed follower of Christ will be stirred to use all of the compassion and urgency he possesses to get individuals into the Word. God wants to speak to us. He wants to show us true riches and life at its best.

Let us pray expectantly that revival will come. When very many people for a very long time look to God for refreshing from above, the Holy Spirit can come like a great wind to clear the air and restore the nation to honor and well-being.

. . . They that wait upon the Lord shall renew their strength, they shall mount up with wings like eagles, they shall run and not be weary, they shall walk and not faint (Isaiah 40:31).

Some spread joy and happiness;
Others just spread!

Conversion is a change of direction;
Repentance is a change of mind;
Revival is change, Christian style!

Do we believe in God the Father Almighty, Maker of heaven and earth?

25

MINISTRY OF SEPARATION

There is a special honor which comes to everyone who becomes a disciple of Christ. He is "chosen . . . out of the world" (John 15:19, KJV). Handpicked! Not because we de-

106

serve it, but because, by yielding to Christ, we make it possible for Him to live in us and to lift our sights above things of the world. ". . . as God said, 'I will live in them and move among them, and I will be their God, and they shall be my people. Therefore come out from them . . . says the Lord . . . and I will be a father to you, and you shall be my sons and daughters, says the Lord Almighty' " (II Corinthians 6:16–17, 18). Come out from the world. Come out of the smog and come into the clear light of God's family!

Once we have been chosen out of the world and have entered the wonder of Christian fellowship and Christian living we in turn are to do all we can to help others to the same separation from the world and its activities.

Let us be sure that we have the right understanding of the word "world." God made everything good, including our globe, but it is evident that world means more than this created ball on which we live. With joy we can sing, "This is my Father's world." Our astronauts described our planet as the good and beautiful earth.

As used by Jesus, world means fallen humanity; the network of persons and forces hostile to Christ. John 3:16 speaks of this world. God so loved fallen humanity that He gave His Son that fallen men and women should not perish. Certainly, He did not love their fallenness, their evil ways. But Christ did die that they might be raised from their fallen state to the glorious state of children of God. We are not to join in their fallenness. Having been saved we are not to love their sinful ways but to turn from them.

"Stop loving this evil world and all that it offers you, for when you love these things you show that you do not really love God; for all these worldly things, these evil desires—the craze for sex, the ambition to buy everything that appeals to you and the pride that comes from wealth and importance— these are not from God. They are from this evil world itself" (I John 2:15–16, LIVING LETTERS). This is the clear call to

107

separation. Paul wrote, ". . . How can right and wrong be partners? What does a believer have in common with an unbeliever? . . . separate yourselves from them" (II Corinthians 6:14–17, TEV).

Mademoiselle Annie Vallotton, who created the unique line drawings in *Today's English Version of the Bible*, did an interesting illustration for this saying of Jesus. With a few strokes of her pen she depicted a group of people composed of three pairs. Each couple is of the same attitude and has the same bearing. The observer quickly sees the need for each figure to break away from the unattractive attitude by separating himself from his partner in order to "be my sons and daughters." (verse 18).

For young people, the call to be different is a most difficult one. To be accepted by their peers is of utmost importance to them. They think acceptance comes by conforming, being just like the rest. They do not dare to heed the call ". . . be not conformed to this world: but be ye transformed . . ." (Romans 12:2, KJV). They think they dare not be different or they will never be happy again. Here is where our ministry of separation must come into play. They need the courage which we can give them. They need to see what is loss and what is gain. With love and much patience, we need to lead them into the Word, into fellowship with other believers so they may see the joy of God's people—so the pleasures of the world will seem strangely dim.

If the world cheats, they must be called to honesty, if the world is self-centered and pleasure-centered, they need to become Christ-centered. If the world is unforgiving, revenge-seeking, they need to learn the blessedness of forgiving. If the worldlings abuse their bodies, they need to remember that their bodies are the temple in which the Holy God dwells.

Not only are we called *away* from the world but *to* a life of service. Paul was "set apart for the gospel." Barnabas and Saul were set apart to do the work to which the Holy Spirit

108

called them. We must not only be different, but must be useful to God. There is work to be done, which only committed followers of Christ can do. How would a man of the world carry the Good News to others, when he has never tasted how good it is? Not until we have a message can we be witnesses.

One word of warning—the call to be separate does not mean that we are not *in* the world. Therefore we must remain as concerned for the world as God was when He sent His son. It does not mean that we are to become holy snobs, holier-than-thou critics. Rather we are to be compassionate ministers, grieved when anyone lives below the high calling he has in Christ, always rejoicing when, through his ministry, another is helped to find a life in which each day is aglow.

Thoughts to Make Your Day Glow

All service ranks the same with God. . . .

ROBERT BROWNING

The most acceptable service of God is doing good to man.

BENJAMIN FRANKLIN

God likes help when helping people.

IRISH PROVERB

V
The Perfect
Consummation

26
STILL IN GOD'S EMPLOY

We began with the assertion that life is aglow when every facet is kindled with light and love from above. But, is this really true as life comes nearer and nearer to its completion? Dare we confine this assertion only to those years when we are at the peak of physical strength and are active in our vocation and in family building? No, man never ceases to want each day to be a good one. In the prime of life it is difficult to imagine that the latter years can be radiantly happy ones, also.

Let me illustrate. I attended the university when I was in my forties. A young woman half my age sat next to me in my psychology class. After weeks of meeting daily in the classroom, she looked me over one morning and ventured the question, "Are you a faculty member?" When I denied being one and admitted that I was only a student as she was, she looked at me with a strange expression. It seemed to say—You poor thing! Why, in your old age, do you still bother to go to school?

Entertaining as it was to be thus evaluated, I couldn't resist opening up her young eyes to a new truth. So I said (I hope with a twinkle in my eye), "Listen, my dear, I want to tell you something and I want you always to remember it. Life gets more wonderful the more it ripens. Each year is better than the one before because of greater knowledge gained, newer insights, deepening experiences. I'm having a wonderful time back at school."

When the girl answered, I was the surprised one. "Oh," she said, "I'm so glad you told me. I have always dreaded the thought of adding years to my life. Thanks so much for relieving me."

Yes, the years of maturity can be aglow. They *can* be, but *are* they so automatically? No, they are only so when each day still has a purpose beyond just staying alive—the purpose God gave to us. We may no longer be employed professionally, but we are still in God's employ. There are duties to be faithfully performed.

There are two special assignments for which we need to be aware. The first is pointed out to us in Psalm 78:3–4: ". . . things that we have heard and known, that our fathers have told us. We will not hide them from their children, but tell to the coming generation the glorious deeds of the Lord, and his might, and the wonders which he has wrought." This thought is repeated in Psalm 73:28: "But for me it is good to be near God; I have made the Lord God my refuge, that I may tell of all thy works." Storytelling is your first assignment in God's employ. You and I are to tell the next generation, children and grandchildren, and great-grandchildren how good it is to trust in the Lord, and what wonderful things He has wrought in our lives. Ask God to make you interesting to young people—winsome and effective in telling how God answered your prayers. Ask God to forgive you if you have not told but kept silent. God has permitted you to reach long life for this very purpose. Be sure to take it seriously.

The second assignment in God's employ is to use your leisure time for prayer. This sin-sick world with all its woes and unhappy people needs prayer desperately. Blessed is the family for which an old father or mother spends hours praying. Such arms of prayer reach up and bring down help and blessing.

In your home, in your community, in the world at large, are those who desperately need to be upheld in intercession. The great tasks of the church succeed in the measure of intercession for them. The peace of the world can come only as enough hearts open to receive peace. Weak souls need to be strengthened; tempted and tested believers need to be undergirded; our national leaders need divine wisdom and guidance; our scientists need direction to find causes and cures for horrible diseases—cancer not the least; workers in our welfare agencies need strength and understanding and patience; missionaries need ability to communicate in new languages; Bible translators need enlightenment to discover new sounds and meanings of words.

You, who have hours of inactivity, are blessed with such hours for folded hands. There is no limit to what you can do, as you cooperate with God in helping men. You ask and He does it (John 14:14). Deep abiding joy will come into your heart with time spent in such employ—God's employ!

Thoughts to Make Your Day Glow

Go home to your friends, and tell them how much the Lord has done for you, and how he has had mercy on you (Mark 5:19).

To live content with small means;
To seek elegance rather than luxury, and refinement rather
    than fashion;
To be worthy, not respectable, and wealthy, not rich;
To study hard, think quietly, talk gently, act frankly;

To listen to stars and birds, to babes and sages, with open
    heart;
To bear all cheerfully, do all bravely, await occasions, hurry
    never.
In a word, to let the spiritual, unbidden and unconscious,
    grow up through the common.
This is to be my symphony.

WILLIAM ELLERY CHANNING

Prayer is the chief agency and activity whereby men
align themselves with God's purpose. Prayer does not con-
sist in battering the walls of heaven for personal benefits
or the success of our plans. Rather is it the committing
of ourselves for the carrying out of His purposes. It is a
telephone call to headquarters for orders. It is not bending
God's will to ours, but our will to God's. In prayer, we
tap vast reservoirs of spiritual power whereby God can find
fuller entrance into the hearts of men.

G. ASHTON OLDHAM

27

THE LAST STRETCH OF THE ROAD

At close of day, when shadows begin to enfold us, the Christian can face home and rest calmly, if Christ lives in his heart.

A friend died recently, and we learned from her family that her last words were, "I am a heavenly passenger." We knew what she meant. Her eyes had been upon her Saviour during her whole lifetime. Throughout her busy, productive professional life, she had lived in the awareness of her Saviour's love. Although the last stretch of the road had been rough, her traveling had been homeward and she had been satisfied. Life still held some joy for her, but home was real to her and it beckoned invitingly. Now her journey is over. All struggle is over and she is enjoying ". . . What no eye has seen, nor ear heard, nor the heart of man conceived, what God has prepared for those who love him" (I Corinthians 2:9). The heavenly passenger has arrived home.

For many years, a certain Scripture passage has given me some trouble. Just what does Psalm 116:15 mean? "Precious in the sight of the Lord is the death of his saints." Could it mean that the life of each heavenly passenger is so valuable, of such consequence to God, that man's death is wonderful, also, because by it man finally enters the very Presence of God? He comes home to stay. This meaning seems to agree with what we read in Revelation 14:13. "And I heard a voice from heaven saying, 'Write this: Blessed are the dead who die in the Lord henceforth.' 'Blessed indeed,' says the Spirit, 'that they may rest from their labors, for their deeds follow them!' "

It is faith-strengthening to hear the words of those to whom a preview of the better world seems to have been given just before they leave this world. This memory can color our lives with brighter hue.

Recently, relatives of a young man, who died many years ago, shared with me the wonderful message he left with them. The thought of that hour has been as a benediction to those who were present at his going. Here is their story.

The young man, in his late twenties, lay critically ill. His dear ones were at his bedside, when he awoke with a start and said, "Oh, I just went so far that I had my choice of going on or coming back."

Someone at his bedside said, "You did right to live."

His reply was unforgettable. He spoke slowly with over-powering conviction and an expression of anticipation, "Oh, no. To die is to live." He had had a foretaste of better things to come and was trying to communicate the wonder of it. He called it *life*! With these words, he entered life. With these words, he sent his dear ones back into daily living. All these years they have used his words as a guiding beacon, which has given them unshakable assurance that to die is to *live*.

A Christian nurse told me about a great Christian leader. Just before he slipped away, his lips were moving, but his voice was soft. As she came closer and listened intently she saw him point upward suddenly and exclaim ecstatically, "Beautiful, Oh, how beautiful." Then he was gone.

Although I heard this story from her many years ago, its glow lives on in my heart. Somehow, I don't mind thinking of the end of the road. It is beautiful. I'm told it is *life*.

Thoughts to Make Your Day Glow

Let Jesus be everything to you
and He will take you home with Him,

118

not only for a day
but forever!

Death is the gate of life.

SAINT BERNARD OF CLAIRVAUX

. . . we can see and understand only a little about God now, as if we were peering at His reflection in a poor mirror; but someday we are going to see Him in His completeness, face to face. Now all that I know is hazy and blurred, but then I will see everything clearly, just as clearly as God sees into my heart right now.

I Corinthians 13:12, LIVING LETTERS

28

THE GREAT ETERNAL DAY

God, in His loving kindness, gave us a glimpse of what we may expect beyond, because He wanted His children to have a radiant hope beyond this age. This hope removes the sting of death. If in spirit we can see ourselves already on that far distant shore, looking back we can see life in the light of eternity.

119

Looking back from there, many of the things to which we devoted our time and effort will seem ridiculous contrasted to things of lasting value, that we neglected. The Christian will do well to evaluate what is really important now and through eternity.

To describe what awaits us yonder is beyond our fondest dreams. Even Scripture could not find adequate words that we could comprehend; the writer of Revelation had to resort to symbolic language.

A special blessing has been promised to all who read and hear this Book. Let us claim this blessing, as we direct our eyes of faith to see what God has prepared and reserved in heaven for those who love Him.

In Chapter 21 our eyes are directed to a city—the new Jerusalem, the holy city. We are not left in doubt as to what this city signifies. The vision is interpreted for us in verses 9 and 10. The holy city is the bride and we know from the epistle writers that the bride is the church, God's people (II Corinthians 11:2, Ephesians 5:21–32). The bride is adorned in all her bridal purity and loveliness. How wonderful it is to realize that God's people shall be free of all ugliness and imperfection because He ". . . loves us and has freed us from our sins by his blood" (Revelation 1:5).

The essential feature of the age to come is that we shall enjoy the Presence of God and fellowship with Him. What a breathtaking experience it will be to finally and actually see Him in whom we have believed, and whom we have only seen with the eyes of faith. This will be heaven—to see Him face to face and be with Him forevermore. ". . . Behold the dwelling of God is with men. He will dwell with them and they shall be his people, and God himself will be with them . . ." (21:3).

". . . and the sea was no more" (21:1) is a simple statement, but it is full of symbolic meaning. Many of us love the majestic rolling waves of the sea, but the Hebrews, a pastoral people, dreaded its terrible power and the awful destruction and devastation it could wreak. When John, the writer of Revelation, was a prisoner on a small bleak, rocky island, the sea seemed an evil thing that surrounded him without hope of escape. The sea symbolizes separation, danger, death. These are not in the holy city. God's people need not fear separation from God. No one and nothing can separate us from the love of Christ Jesus (Romans 8:35-39).

But banishment of all that saddens and clouds life (Revelation 21:4) is wonderful also. No more tears, death, mourning, crying, pain—this is too good to comprehend.

The greatness and perfection of the city is expressed by giving its measurements—its heighth, breadth, and length. We find that it is the measurement of a cube. The square and the cube have been regarded as symbols of perfection. Twelve is a number of completeness in the Bible. A cube is twelve times twelve times twelve, which is another way of indicating the perfection of God's people when they are in His Presence, made holy by the Lamb's blood.

The wall, too, is measured and it was "a great, high wall . . ." (21:12)—a symbol of security, of protection from threat or attack by Satan. We won't even need to try to be good, because we shall be as He is when we are in his Presence (I John 3:2). And we need never expect to be defeated by Satan's temptations; he will have been destroyed. The wall symbolizes the final and eternal union and communion of God with all who are His own.

Even the foundations of the wall of the city are described; they are garnished with all manner of precious stones. Gems are among the most durable substances known to man, fit symbols of the Word of the Lord, which lives and abides and endures forever (I Peter 1:23-25). Jesus Himself said, "Heaven and earth will pass away, but my words will not pass away" (Matthew 24:35). And as the stones in the foundation of the holy city are beautiful and precious, so is the Word of God precious and beautiful beyond compare.

Each of the gates was made of a single pearl (Revelation

121

21:21). Gates are the symbol of entrance—but why made of pearl? To understand its symbolism, we need to ask what is a pearl? We know is as a smooth, hard, roundish growth formed around a foreign body within the shell of a mollusk—usually an oyster. Let us say that a grain of sand somehow gets into the innards of the oyster. To ease the irritation—the destructive working of the sand—the oyster covers the sand particle with layers of slime. When we open the oyster and find this pain remover, we say, "Look, I found a pearl." ". . . through many tribulations we must enter the kingdom of God" (Acts 14:22).

The expression, "streets of gold," is familiar to most people, but what is the meaning hidden behind this symbol? Gold has always been the symbol of that which is most precious. For us, love is the most precious ingredient for happy living. Streets are symbolical of interaction, communication, fellowship, living together. Thus, in the holy city, God's people will have fellowship and meet each other in the most precious way—in love. We shall walk together in love.

There is no temple in the city (21:22). In Old Testament days, the temple was a place of Sabbath meeting, of holy convocation with God. In the holy city, God will be right there with His people—not only on Sabbath days, but forever. A meeting place is no longer needed. We shall enjoy the everlasting meeting with Him, on the everlasting Lord's day.

"And there shall be no night there." This is mentioned twice: Once, as a reason why the gates of the city never need be closed—access to God is always possible. The second time it is mentioned it implies that our service in heaven need never be interrupted by darkness. There is a divine source of unfailing light: ". . . for the glory of God is its light" (21:23).

John was overwhelmed by what he had seen and heard. As we contemplate such a glorious future, we, too, shall be overwhelmed when the "Day Eternal" dawns and we are *home*.

Thoughts to Make Your Day Glow

Jerusalem, thou city fair and high,
    Would God I were in thee!
My longing heart fain, fain to thee would fly,
    It will not stay with me.
Far over vale and mountain,
    Far over field and plain,
It hastes to seek its fountain
    And quit this world of pain.

O happy day, and yet far happier hour,
    When wilt thou come at last?
When fearless to my Father's love and power,
    Whose promise standeth fast,
My soul I gladly render
    For surely will his hand
Lead her, with guidance tender
    To heaven her fatherland.

JOHAN MATTAUS MAYVART

How vast is eternity!

NATHANIEL EMMONS

He who has no vision of eternity has no hold on time.

THOMAS CARLYLE